EXCELLENCE

IN

MINISTRY

By Robb Thompson

Excellence in Ministry
ISBN 1-889723-22-3
Copyright © 2002 by Robb Thompson
Family Harvest Church
18500 92nd Ave.
Tinley Park, Illinois 60477

Editorial Consultant: Cynthia Hansen
Text Design: Lisa Simpson
Cover Design: Greg Lane

Second Printing, 2003

Dedication

I would like to dedicate this book to the pastoral staff of Family Harvest Church in Chicago, Illinois, USA. I so appreciate their never-ending ability to pursue excellence in the ever-changing world of ministering to the most valuable commodity on the face of the earth — *God's people.*

I particularly want to thank:

- Doug Boettcher
- Mark Friend
- Mike Kell
- John Paladino
- Patty Plante
- Mary Beth Pozdol
- Nancy Shannon

Thank you for making my life so much easier.

TABLE OF CONTENTS

ACKNOWLEDGMENT

I would like to give a special thanks to Pastor Robert Kayanja for his deep love and commitment to his native land of Uganda. It is to him that this great African nation owes the writing of this book, as well as my involvement in both its present and its future.

FOREWORD

Excellence is an anointing from Heaven just as miracle healing is. It is also one of the most important character traits of our Father God. In all my twenty years of ministry, I have never seen such a unique gift of excellence as exemplified in the life, ministry, words, and family of Pastor Robb Thompson.

When I first had the privilege of meeting and observing this man of God, I said to myself, *I would have Robb Thompson as my teacher. I want him to take me to that level of excellence where he lives.* Since then, I have fellowshipped with him casually in his home and I have been with him in his church, and I can say this with certainty: *What Pastor Robb teaches is just an overflow of the person he truly is.*

My home is in Africa — a continent that desperately needs this gift of excellence on all levels of life: governmental and educational, in churches and in homes. Robb Thompson is an instrument God is using to further this goal. Largely because of this man of God, the "Never Again" project has become a reality to meet the practical and spiritual needs of the street children and orphans of Kampala.

This is a must-read book. The principles of excellence contained within its pages are steps you have to take if your ministry is to become a ministry of excellence — full of miracles and multitudes won for the Kingdom of God, making a mark that will last throughout all eternity.

I am so grateful to Pastor Robb for authoring this book. It is a vital key to releasing greatness in the African revival, as well as in the revival of the Church worldwide!

Pastor Robert Kayanja
Miracle Centre Cathedral
Kampala, Uganda

INTRODUCTION

When I was still a young Christian, I used to sit in church and look at the minister who stood behind the pulpit, wondering, *How can I get from where I am right now to where he is?* I'd listen to the minister tell about all the wonderful things God had done in his life, and I'd think, *I'm looking for that kind of testimony in my own life!*

I had already learned from the Word of God that I didn't have to live the same low-level way I had learned while growing up. But I still had to figure out what it was going to take to change me so I could be all God had created me to be. I knew that change was absolutely essential if I was ever going to fulfill the call He had placed on my life to the ministry.

That's what I want to talk to you about, my friend. If you sense a divine call to the ministry, I want to share with you the discovery I made that took me beyond all my yesterdays into my God-ordained destiny as a minister of the Gospel. Once you make that same discovery, you'll wonder what took you so long to find this missing piece of the puzzle in your walk with God!

The essence of my discovery is simple: *You have to live with an inner drive to pursue excellence every day of your life.* Now, I'm not saying you *have* to make that choice. You can actually decide to go through life being ordinary, just like everyone else.

But if you choose to be like everyone else, you will never become what God wants you to be. You will never be successful in fulfilling your call to the ministry. That would be an eternal tragedy, for there are people on the earth whom God has specifically ordained *you* to reach with the love of God and the message of salvation through Jesus Christ.

Psalms 11:3 says, **"If the foundations are destroyed, what can the righteous do?"** In other words, the psalmist is asking the question: "What can we do when we see the very foundations of our community and our country being destroyed by the strategies of the enemy?" I'll tell you what we can do: *We can continue to press into God.* As we do, we will help lay a deep foundation of godliness and excellence that will become the source of all that God desires to bring forth in our nation and in the lives of the people we serve.

So I challenge you to see how far you can press into greatness. Don't settle for anything less than **"...the prize of the high calling of God in Christ Jesus"** (Phil. 3:14 *KJV*). As you diligently follow God's principles of excellence in every aspect of your life and ministry, He will take you to a higher realm of ministering in His power than you ever imagined was possible. Fruit will come forth in your life that will not only bless you, but everyone around you. And God will use you mightily to build His Kingdom in your church, your community, your country — even to the ends of the earth!

Robb Thompson

REACHING BEYOND YOUR YESTERDAYS

The call of God first comes to you like the promise of a peaceful summer morning. You know the kind of morning I'm talking about. You wake up while the dew is still on the grass and the sun is just peeking over the horizon, streaming its first new rays into your bedroom. You throw open the windows to let the early morning breeze freshen the house; and you think, *This is the day I've been waiting for. It's going to be a WONDERFUL day!*

That's what it's like when you first sense God's call to the ministry. You are flooded with thoughts of the goodness of God and an excitement to embrace the future. You see greatness on the horizon. You anticipate the wonderful years that are to come upon you as you answer the call.

But as you launch out into the ministry, you discover that answering the call isn't anything like you thought it would be. It begins to dawn on you that your fresh, early summer morning has become a very hot summer day!

It's when you're sweltering in the heat of the day — when obstacles, opposition, disillusionment, and adversities seem to hit you from every side — that you must not lose sight of the greatness that still looms on the horizon. That distant goal is not a mirage or an illusion; it's the vision God Himself has placed in your heart. However, greatness will never be thrust upon you automatically; it is something that must be forcefully *pursued* through a lifetime of continued progress.

This is exactly why God has provided you with principles of excellence from His Word — principles that will hold you steady and keep you going strong in the heat of the day when it seems so tempting to give up and find some cool, dark shadows to hide in. But understand this: These principles will not help you if you view them as just another list of mental information to store away. *You must actively apply them to your life every moment of every day.*

You see, excellence in ministry is a *journey*, not a *destination*. You'll never officially "arrive" at the greatness you see on the horizon, and God doesn't expect you to. All He requires of you is that you continually follow His principles of excellence, always striving toward the mark of the prize of your high calling in Christ Jesus. As you do, you will draw ever closer to the day when the Master says those words your heart longs to hear: *"Well done, thou good and faithful servant."*

Break the Power of Yesterday

The principles of excellence God has given you are the basis by which you can change your future and determine the outcome for your life. God spoke forth and then moved upon men to record what He said in His Word. Now He leaves it up to you to discover His principles and follow them all the way to your God-ordained destiny. This is especially important when you sense His call to the ministry, for I know of no greater honor than to serve in God's Kingdom as a minister to His people.

Despite the honor of such a divine call, many people come up with excuses for ignoring the call to the ministry that they sense in their hearts. They make the mistake of becoming "excusiologists," using all kinds of excuses for being non-achievers. For instance, they might say:

- "My national heritage hinders me."
- "I had a difficult childhood."
- "I'm not of the favored race."
- "I don't have enough money."
- "I was born on the wrong side of the tracks."

These excuses can go on indefinitely, but they always reflect the attitude of the excusiologist: "All these circumstances are just wrong, wrong, wrong, wrong, wrong. If only they were right, right, right, right, right, everything would be different, different, different, different, different for me."

But it doesn't really matter where you came from or what color you are. There are advantages and disadvantages to every person's genetic and environmental background. You just need to be smart enough and sensitive enough to the Holy Spirit to understand *your* advantages and then walk through the doors of opportunity that open for you in life.

Before you can do that, however, you must knock out of your life the demonic forces that already caused defeat in the lives of your parents, your grandparents, and everyone else who came before you in your family lineage and in society as a whole. If you *don't* get rid of those demons, they will knock you out as well, and you'll end up no better off than your predecessors.

You see, your life is a culmination of approximately four hundred years of family history, for Numbers 14:18 says that the sins of the fathers are passed down unto the third and fourth generations. That means every sin, every problem, and every stronghold that your ancestors struggled with have been passed down from generation to generation, and over the years you have had to deal with them in your own life. The temptations and the wrong desires that torment you at times are the manifestation of four generations of sin. They are all a part of what I call your "genetic determinism."

Have you known anyone to whom bad things keep happening, and you could never figure out why? It was just time for the harvest to come from the seeds planted in that family line.

We are all in a race against time, friend. What you do, what you think, how you act, and the way you treat people will always produce a harvest — if not in your life, then in the lives of your children. That means someone has to pay the price so your children can live free of all the generational baggage — and that someone is you!

It is of utmost importance that you break the power of yesterday in your life. You must determine to go beyond and do more than those who have come before you. You don't have to live like your daddy and your momma lived. You don't have to be the way your teachers taught you to be in school. You've been made a new creature in Christ. You have a new Father, and according to Titus 3:5, that new Father "re-engineered" you!

Not by works of righteousness which we have done, but according to His mercy HE SAVED US, THROUGH THE WASHING OF REGENERATION and renewing of the Holy Spirit.

You are a new creature in Christ; your past has been wiped away. But you won't enjoy the benefits of that fact until you start *acting* like a new creature!

Now, you have to understand that whenever you go beyond the mediocre norm in life, it's painful. But at least you're the one who is choosing the moment of pain. If you don't choose the moment of pain in your life, it will be chosen for you at a time when it's much less convenient.

I know what I'm talking about. You see, I came from a family background of welfare, eviction, witchcraft, alcoholism, and drug addiction. There didn't seem to be any way in the world for me to escape my already-determined destiny. The devil had set the course of my life. He had been working on my ultimate failure for at least four hundred years!

But I recognized something when I was still an unsaved teenager: *I didn't want to be like where I had come from.* I loved my grandma and grandpa, but I didn't want to be like them. I loved my mom and dad, but I didn't want to be like them either.

However, even back then I knew I would get the same results my parents got if I did the same things my parents did. I couldn't supercede their lives until I did something different than they had done with their lives.

I realized I had to take hold of my life and change *me*, because no one else was going to do it for me. I certainly couldn't expect my parents to change me. They didn't have the knowledge I needed to become a better person. In order to go beyond where I had come from, I would have to find another source to access the knowledge I needed.

After going down quite a few wrong paths in search of that other source — paths that eventually led me to a mental institution! — I finally found my answer in Jesus. Once I found my answer, I decided it was all or nothing. I wouldn't let myself be a mediocre Christian. I was going to pursue Jesus with all my heart.

That choice is the reason my life has turned out the way it has. When I first got saved, I never thought for a moment that I might ever enter the ministry. I never imagined that one day I might be someone whom people around the world would recognize and listen to. I never set out to achieve fame or recognition, and I still don't desire that. Nevertheless, these blessings have come upon me as a result of specific decisions I have made over the years.

Perhaps you, too, come from a difficult background. In the past, the world may have dealt you a death blow. You may have been told that you can't make it in ministry and that you are doomed to fail.

But focus only on what *God* tells you. He says that greater is He who is in you than he that is in the world (John 4:4). He says that you are born of Him and therefore can overcome the world by your faith (1 John 5:4).

God has never said to you, "Well, you know, you were born on the wrong side of the tracks, so you're not going to make it. You were never meant to succeed in what I've called you to do." If those lies have been bombarding your mind, you need to realize where they're coming from. Certainly they aren't coming from God!

God made us all winners; He didn't leave out even one of us. Remember what He said in Galatians 3:26,28:

For you are ALL sons of God through faith in Christ Jesus....

There is neither Jew nor Greek, there is neither slave nor free, there is neither male nor female; for you are ALL one in Christ Jesus.

Please believe me when I tell you this: In redemption, it doesn't matter what your background is. It doesn't matter what nationality or race you are. You have been called by God to live above the world's ideas and prejudices. He has provided a place for you to dwell far above the things of the world, hidden in the secret place of His Presence where fear cannot come and where every God-given dream can be realized.

As a child of God through faith in the Lord Jesus Christ, you are an heir according to the promise. So don't ever let anyone tell you that you weren't meant to win! God has called you to win. *He has created you to be a bearer of the One who created the universe with the words of His mouth.*

Therefore, it doesn't matter what anyone says or thinks about you. It doesn't matter if people say you are at a disadvantage because you don't have the necessary background or education or training or experience. You may have been surrounded your entire life by people who failed to realize their dreams, but that doesn't mean *you* have to fail.

I made the decision long ago that it doesn't matter how I was raised. It doesn't matter who you think I am. I'm serving you notice right now — you are going to see me win! You may not be able to see the full manifestation of my victory right now, but just hide in the bushes and watch — because I'm going to win!

Don't think for one minute that I'm going to breathe and not win. It takes just as much effort to breathe and *lose* as it does to breathe and *win*, and I'm not a loser!

You have to develop the same confident trust in God's ability to bring you to the greatness you see on the horizon of your life. It doesn't matter what other people think or say about it. All that matters is what *God* has said and what you believe about yourself. God says that promotion comes from Him (Ps. 75:6,7). He also says that as you think in your heart, so are you (Prov. 23:7).

So what do you think about yourself? Perhaps you focus on the way you look on the outside, thinking, *You know, you're so unworthy. You can't make it. You're too stupid. You just can't get on top of things, can you? It works for everyone else, but it has never worked for you.*

I guarantee you, friend, those kind of thoughts aren't going to help you realize your dream of fulfilling your divine call with excellence. But I'll tell you what *will* help: *A quality choice on your part to believe what God says about you and to aggressively pursue His principles of ministerial excellence every day of your life.*

It's Your Choice

You see, life is a series of *choices*, not a series of *chances*. When you make a decision to go in a certain direction, that decision will often play out in your life over the next thirty years or more. That means you are experiencing today the results of choices you made years ago. One day you'll look back and realize how different your life would have been if you had just made one small adjustment in some of the decisions you made so many years ago.

So if God has called you to the ministry and you haven't yet said yes, don't make excuses for yourself. That's in essence what Elijah told Elisha when it was Elisha's turn to answer the call. Let's look at the account in First Kings 19:15-20:

> **Then the Lord said to him: "Go, return on your way to the Wilderness of Damascus; and when you arrive, anoint Hazael as king over Syria.**
>
> **"Also you shall anoint Jehu the son of Nimshi as king over Israel. And Elisha the son of Shaphat of Abel Meholah you shall anoint as prophet in your place.**
>
> **"It shall be that whoever escapes the sword of Hazael, Jehu will kill; and whoever escapes the sword of Jehu, Elisha will kill.**
>
> **"Yet I have reserved seven thousand in Israel, all whose knees have not bowed to Baal, and every mouth that has not kissed him."**

So he departed from there, and found Elisha the son of Shaphat, who was plowing with twelve yoke of oxen before him, and he was with the twelfth. Then Elijah passed by him and threw his mantle on him.

And he left the oxen and ran after Elijah, and said, "Please let me kiss my father and my mother, and then I will follow you." And he said to him, "Go back again, for what have I done to you?"

Elijah threw his cloak over Elisha to symbolize God's call to the ministry on the younger man's life. But Elisha said, "Now, wait a second, Elijah. I have some things I have to do first. I'll be very busy getting these matters straightened out, so if you could just hang around, I'll be ready as soon as I can."

But Elijah just looked at him and said in effect, "Look, Elisha, if I'm the one who is calling you, we can have a discussion about this. But if *God* is calling you, you better stop the excuses!"

It's a choice we all have to make — whether or not we're going to obey what God has called us to do in this life. I remember the day I made that choice for myself. I had no personal desire to go into the ministry. On my own, I would have probably moved toward a career in business. I could have told everyone who was relying on my obedience to God's call, "Hey, you're just going to have to make it to Heaven someway or another on your own!"

But I decided that I should at least commit myself to pursuing the call to the ministry for a certain amount of time. Well, that certain amount of time just kept extending and extending — until pretty soon there was no end in sight! But it all started with a choice to obey.

The Choice To Pursue

As a leader, I have observed over the years what happens to many people after they receive the Lord. At first, they're so turned on to Jesus that they just don't know what to do. You can't keep them out of church. They volunteer for everything. But then from the moment they get saved, their lives begin to descend. Instead of intensifying their walk with God, they begin to make compromises. They begin to take steps backwards in the commitment they made toward God. And in the end, they find out that less commitment brings less multiplication and considerably less blessing.

People who go backwards in their walk with God like that just don't love Him enough. That's why they start compromising. That's why they say, "I think it's legalistic to say you need to go to church every time the doors are open."

I've had people say things like that to me a lot through the years. But it isn't legalistic to be in church all the time when you're so much in love with God that you just can't stay away!

The further I've gone in my Christian walk, the more I've realized that I might as well not worry about other people viewing me as legalistic. I can't let my life be controlled by people who aren't going to do what is right anyway. Why should I keep backing up — making less and less requirements on myself and others — in order to conform to someone else's lower standards? Then everyone would end up as a mediocre Christian!

You see, choices are a lordship issue. God must be first in your life. If He is first in your life, that means He is first in how you choose to spend your time. It means that His call on your life is the course you choose to pursue.

You won't succeed in life until you embrace that divine call and begin to fulfill it with excellence. You must push off your past and get rid of your yesterdays. If you don't dump all that baggage, you'll be hopelessly sidetracked. You simply cannot carry the baggage of the past into your future and succeed.

You must always remember that there is no future in your past. You cannot go forward when you're always looking through the rearview mirror. The only way you can maintain a forward progress in life is to walk by faith and not by sight (2 Cor. 5:7).

But although you can't go backwards and fix where you have been, you *can* fix where you are now by sowing the right seeds for your future. Those good seeds of obedience will begin to take root and eventually produce a great harvest of blessing not only in your life, but in the lives of those you minister to.

However, you must believe in where you are headed in life, not in where you used to be. You must walk by that which God says, not by that which you see with your natural eyes. As Second Corinthians 4:18 (*KJV*) says, **"...We look not at the things which are seen, but at the things which are not seen: for the things which are seen are temporal; but the things which are not seen are eternal."**

So start praying for excellence as you answer God's call to the ministry. Cultivate your inner drive to pursue excellence with all your strength. Determine to reach beyond your yesterdays so you can take hold of your God-ordained tomorrows. Go beyond every devil you've ever faced before, and pick a new fight in a bigger ring — namely, your future as a minister in the Kingdom of God!

NOTES:

_____

_____

_____

_____

_____

_____

_____

_____

NOTES:

PREPARING FOR THE CALL WITH EXCELLENCE

There is always a day of preparation that brings you to the day when you are separated unto the call God has placed on your life. This was certainly true in the apostle Paul's life.

Acts 13:1-4 relates the time Barnabus and Saul (soon to be called Paul) were separated unto the ministry as apostles to the Gentiles. Up to this point, Barnabus was the head of the ministry team, and both men had been used greatly in the field to minister the Gospel to others. However, the Holy Spirit hadn't yet declared what ministry office Barnabus and Paul had been called to fulfill — not until one day when the prophets and elders came together to fast and pray. Then the Holy Spirit spoke:

...*"Now separate to Me Barnabas and Saul for the work to which I have called them.*"
Then, having fasted and prayed, and laid hands on them, they sent them away.

So, being sent out by the Holy Spirit, they went down to Seleucia, and from there they sailed to Cyprus.
Acts 13:2-4

Before that time, Paul hadn't been separated unto the ministry God had called him to fulfill as an apostle to the Gentiles. He was in his preparatory stages. The Holy Spirit was working within him to get him ready for a ministry of excellence.

It's so important to understand this. In between the call of God and the separation, a time of preparation must take place. Too many people are failing in ministry today because they never understood this principle and have messed up their ministries as a result.

As soon as these people sensed God's call on their lives, they went out and attempted to minister in the power of the Holy Spirit. But they fell flat on their faces because they never prepared. They never sat under the ministry of a man or woman of God to whom they had been assigned. They never sat in the classroom of the Holy Spirit. Spiritual elders never laid their hands on them to separate them unto the ministry. Yet they still thought they could go out in that sad condition and fulfill a ministry of excellence!

It doesn't work that way. Preparation is absolutely vital to a successful ministry. It must include the experience and the schooling you need in order to become everything God desires for you to be. That might mean getting a college education at a university or a Bible college. Certainly it means serving under a minister of God in the local church, helping to further the Kingdom of God in the community you live in.

In light of all this, I want to share with you several principles of excellence that will help you successfully prepare for *your* personal "prize of the high calling of God in Christ Jesus."

AN EXCELLENT MINISTER UNDERSTANDS THAT GOD HAS ALREADY SCHEDULED HIS MOMENT FOR SEPARATION UNTO THE CALL, BUT HE MUST READY HIMSELF FOR THAT MOMENT.

Timing is very important to you. This very day you are determining whether or not you will be ready for the next season God has planned for you by your willingness or your unwillingness to prepare for it.

You see, the will of God is constant and continually flowing throughout eternity. It is only when you actually converge with God's will that you can receive it. However, if your moment of divine purpose comes and you haven't prepared, you won't be ready to receive God's will for you. That divine purpose will move on to someone else who *is* ready, and you will be left behind.

> AN EXCELLENT MINISTER PURSUES THE CHANGE
> THAT WILL PREPARE HIM FOR THE FUTURE.

Instead of always wanting your circumstances or the people around you to change, you must be willing for God to change you on a daily basis. Only then can you become the kind of vessel through which the Holy Spirit can freely minister to others.

In Second Corinthians 3:18, the Bible tells us what God wants for His people:

But we all, with unveiled face, beholding as in a mirror the glory of the Lord, are being transformed into the same image from glory to glory, just as by the Spirit of the Lord.

It is God's plan for His people to continually be in a state of transformation as they become more and more like Jesus. Unfortunately, the vast majority of Christians refuse to change. They want their situations to change, but they themselves do not want to change. In fact, statistics show that in America, more than ninety-three percent of the population refuses change.

You can't be like that if you want to be an excellent minister. You must embrace change every day so you can be significant not only in the lives of those you serve, but in the heart and the mind of

God as He leads you into the fullness of what He has planned for you.

> **AN EXCELLENT MINISTER CHOOSES
> TO DISMANTLE HIS LIFE IN TIMES
> WHEN HE CAN WITHSTAND THE PAIN OF CHANGE.**

Change just cannot happen until you choose to dismantle the unnecessary things in your life that hinder you from pursuing your call.

Sometimes that's difficult. It isn't easy to let go of activities, commitments, relationships, and interests that are producing negative fruit in your life. But if you don't systematically dismantle these negative things and eliminate them from your life one at a time when it's convenient, the day will come when the harvest of negative fruit will dismantle *you*. And I guarantee you this: When that day comes, it *won't* be at a convenient time for you!

> **AN EXCELLENT MINISTER
> EMBRACES SHORT-TERM DENIAL IN ORDER
> TO CREATE LONG-TERM BENEFITS.**

Remember this: People who are losers in life always go for short-term pleasure. On the other hand, a person who is a winner in life always chooses short-term denial in order to enjoy long-term pleasure.

This goes along with being willing to dismantle any unnecessary weights that hinder you in your walk with God. Many people in life want to enjoy the short-term benefits of those "weights" right now; therefore, these people refuse to deny themselves, even though they may suffer for their choice in the future.

But if you desire to be an excellent minister, you must always choose to accept short-term self-denial so that, years down the road, you will be able to obtain your long-term desires and enjoy the long-term pleasure you want to achieve for yourself, for your family, and for the ministry God has called you to fulfill.

AN EXCELLENT MINISTER UNDERSTANDS THAT LASTING CHANGE REQUIRES ROOTING OUT YESTERDAY'S PAIN IN ORDER TO EXPERIENCE RELIEF FROM YESTERDAY'S MEMORIES.

I remember hearing about a man who always asked people the question, "Who has most influenced your life?"

People would often name their mother, father, or spiritual leader in response to that question. But this man would always reply, "That isn't true. *The one who has influenced your life the most is the one who has caused you the most amount of pain.*"

Whether you realize it or not, you are living your life responding to the pain you have faced in days gone by. That's why you shy away from putting yourself in certain situations or dealing with certain people.

So make the decision to root out yesterday's pain; then let it go once and for all. Allow the Holy Spirit complete access to your heart so He can heal you and make you whole. Otherwise, you'll keep reacting to situations according to the pain that still festers inside and will never become all that God wants you to become in your life and ministry.

> **AN EXCELLENT MINISTER ALWAYS BUILDS HIS LIFE ON A FIRM FOUNDATION.**

Everything you believe, everything you do, and everything you are in life must always have a strong scriptural foundation underneath it in order to be successful. That's why Jesus said this in Luke 6:46-49:

> **"But why do you call Me 'Lord, Lord,' and do not do the things which I say?**
> **"Whoever comes to Me, and hears My sayings and does them, I will show you whom he is like:**
> **"He is like a man building a house, who dug deep and laid the foundation on the rock. And when the flood arose, the stream beat vehemently against that house, and could not shake it, for it was founded on the rock.**
> **"But he who heard and did nothing is like a man who built a house on the earth**

without a foundation, against which the stream beat vehemently; and immediately it fell. And the ruin of that house was great."

The first man dug deep and then built his house on a foundation of solid rock. Whenever the floods came and the winds blew, that man's house always stood firm because it was built on a strong foundation. The second man, however, built his house on level ground with no foundation. When the storms of life blew against his house, it collapsed and was blown away.

Personally, I make sure that everything over which God has given me responsibility in my life has a strong foundation of the Word of God underneath it. I can tell you why I believe everything I believe. I can tell you why I allow my family members to do what they do, say what they say, and live as they live.

Because every aspect of my life is built on the solid foundation of God's Word, I am ready to come through every storm victoriously as I fulfill my call to the ministry. The same should be true for all of us.

AN EXCELLENT MINISTER LIVES LIFE BY HIS PRINCIPLES, NOT BY HIS EMOTIONS.

So many people live by their feelings, and that includes ministers all over the world. These people respond to every situation according to what they think or feel about that situation, not according to what God says in His Word about it. Their emotions become the standard by which they act.

But you must go beyond that. You have to change from living an *emotional* life to living a *principle-centered* life. How do you accomplish this?

- By continually striving to become like Jesus, who is your greatest Example of an excellent minister.

- By obeying the same principles set forth in God's Word that you expect everyone else to obey, even when your mind doesn't understand why.

- By holding on to those principles, knowing they are the very underpinnings of the strong foundation upon which you have built your life and ministry.

AN EXCELLENT MINISTER KNOWS THAT TESTING IS REQUIRED FOR PROMOTION.

You never go to the next grade in school until you've passed the tests of the last grade. The same is true in every area of your life, including your call to the ministry. When you pass the intermediate tests in your season of preparation, God takes you on to advanced testing to see what your potential is in the Kingdom of God.

Many Christians assume it's God's will for them to escape every difficult situation that arises in their lives. For instance, someone once told me, "I've been having such a rough time at my job lately!"

"Oh, really? What's been going on?" I asked.

"Oh, the people I work with don't like me. They even told me that they hate me! I think God is moving me on."

"Let me ask you something," I replied. "Who do you think went with Daniel into the lions' den? Daniel didn't say, 'Hey, wait a minute! I know the Lord can't be leading me into this lions' den!' Daniel knew that sometimes God allows His people to stay in difficult situations to see if they pass the test!"

Remember, the Bible says Jesus was led *of the Spirit* into the wilderness to be tempted by the devil (Matt. 4:1). You see, before you can come back in the power of the Spirit, you have to go to the wilderness. Now, you don't have to go there the same way Jesus did, because He has already defeated the enemy. But you *will* have to face and conquer your own wilderness — and that wilderness is *you*!

One of the greatest challenges you will ever face in your life is the challenge of the Goliath that lives inside your carnal nature. Yes, you have to deal with Satan and his demons, but the greatest enemy you will ever face is yourself.

Every day you must pursue, overtake, and conquer yourself so the Holy Spirit can live His life through you. Jesus said it like this: **"For even the Son of Man did not come to be served, but to serve, and to give His life a ransom for many"** (Mark 10:45).

So ask yourself each morning:

- *Will I let myself be the greatest enemy I'll ever face this day?*

- *Am I willing to humble myself?*

- *Am I willing to lay my life down so God can give it back to me again?*

- *Am I willing to serve the people I don't want to serve?*

- *Am I willing to give when I don't want to give?*

- *Am I willing to bless when I don't want to bless?*

- *Am I willing to focus on becoming what I need to become for others, instead of focusing on what I want others to be for me?*

Why is it so important to conquer your own carnal nature? Because the devil is trying to make you disqualify yourself for what God has for you in the ministry. The enemy will bring situations into your life designed to keep you from reaching the prize on the other side of the mountain. He wants you to say, "You know, all this preparation is just too much. I can't take it anymore!"

Keep in mind what Jesus told you about the devil: **"The thief does not come except to steal, and to kill, and to destroy..."** (John 10:10). There is a thief that speaks to you every day. He tries to keep you from going God's way, from going beyond the norm — beyond what is acceptable to other people. He attempts to keep you from attaining excellence by convincing you that you don't want to stand out in the crowd.

That voice is intent on killing greatness within you. If you listen to it, that voice will steal the destiny God wants you to reach in life. It will destroy the future Jesus paid with His blood to give you — a future full of life, super-abundant in quantity and superior in quality (John 10:10).

You see, with each new day, the score of the game you are in reverts back to "Christian — 0; Satan — 0." But God has made sure that *you are the winner in this game.* That's why you have to wake up every morning with the thought, *What ground am I going to take back from what the devil has stolen from me?* And it isn't just a matter of taking back the ground the devil has already stolen from you in the past. You must also make sure he doesn't gain the ground he wants to steal from you that very day!

The Bible says that when a thief is caught, he must restore sevenfold what he has stolen (Prov. 6:31). That means you have the authority and the covenant right in Jesus' Name to demand that the devil restore to you sevenfold all he has ever stolen from you. If you will do that each day by faith, you'll always go to bed at night one step further than you were the day before — and the devil will have the losing score!

AN EXCELLENT MINISTER KNOWS THAT TODAY'S EXCELLENCE IS TOMORROW'S MEDIOCRITY.

Make the decision, "My excellence of today is as far back as I'm going to go for my tomorrow. I will never go back any further than the level of excellence I have attained today."

You see, you have to understand when the timing is right for you to begin to make a move for you to become better. Once you make that move, you then have the challenge of holding your ground at the higher level to which you have attained.

So hold on, my friend. Every step forward you take, drive a stake in the ground where you stand and say, "I will never go back any further than where I am right now!" Even if you run into a storm and it becomes very difficult to hold fast to the ground you have gained, don't ever take a step backwards. If you do, I guarantee you that you will face that storm again, and next time it will be harder.

AN EXCELLENT MINISTER IS CONVINCED THAT EVERY STEP AWAY FROM TEMPTATION IS ONE STEP CLOSER TO GOD'S DREAM WITHIN HIM.

You must remember this: Every time the devil offers you something, you have a new opportunity to say to him, "Get thee behind me, Satan!" When you do that, the devil will leave you for more opportune moment, as he did with Jesus in Matthew 4 — but you can keep him from ever finding one! You can choose every day to walk away from the things of this world. As you do, the things of Heaven will come to you in a greater and greater measure.

AN EXCELLENT MINISTER KNOWS THAT OBEDIENCE TO THE KNOWN WILL OF GOD IS THE KEY TO UNLOCKING HIS UNKNOWN WILL.

The known will of God is laid out plainly in the Scriptures, telling you how to respond in every area of your life. Before God will ever reveal to you His unknown will — the fullness of what He has called you to do in this life — you must first obey His known will, which is found in the Word of God.

For instance, God's Word tells you that you need to tithe. When you bring ten percent of your income to the Lord, He promises to rebuke the devourer from your life (Mal. 3:10,11). There are no ifs, ands, or buts about this divine command to tithe; it is just one of God's instructions you must obey in order to advance further in your pursuit of excellence.

God's Word also tells you in Isaiah 1:19 that, if you are willing and obedient, you will eat the best of the land. This lets you know that you can't eat the good of the land, nor can you even begin to qualify for the ministry, until you have first determined to be obedient.

> ### AN EXCELLENT MINISTER ESTABLISHES GOD'S PRINCIPLES IN HIS LIFE ONE STEP AT A TIME.

Get rid of peripheral things in your life that bog down your forward progress; meanwhile, work on establishing one principle of excellence at a time on the inside of you. You see, it takes time to establish these principles in your heart. Life isn't accomplished all at once; you have to take it step by step.

So be careful not to try to change everything in your life that needs changing in a short period of time. Don't get in a hurry. Just be determined to take back more ground every day. Pick one area in your life to fix, and then fix that one thing. When you've mastered that one area, you can go on to the next one — but only after you have mastered what you have already tackled.

However, although it's true you have to pursue excellence step by step, you shouldn't procrastinate in taking those steps. One thing you do not have is an excessive amount of time. You can't afford to wait to fix problems in your life because, in light of eternity, you only have a small slice of time to live on this earth. At the same time, you have all kinds of divine assignments you're supposed to fulfill within the time that is left to you.

On the other hand, Satan is an eternal being. Because he isn't a time-and-space being, he has a lot of time to work on you. That's the reason you can be most effective in life by focusing on one area at a time all the way to completion before you go on to fix the next area.

Use a step-by-step process in everything you do to make sure you're ready to make any necessary change. Develop a lifestyle that doesn't constantly move *from miracle to miracle*, but rather *from faith to faith*. Remember, excellence — *not* miracles — is the currency of God's Kingdom.

> **AN EXCELLENT MINISTER USES FOCUS TO DELIVER HIM TO HIS GOD-GIVEN DESTINATION.**

Once you lock in your focus on a particular goal to achieve, don't change. Keep your focus unbroken until you reach the goal that is set before you.

Broken focus is one of the greatest enemies of excellence. You see, there is great joy to be found in completing a task. However, ministers often live their lives in continual disappointment because so many tasks they start don't get finished. As a result, these ministers live from one day to the next without a sense of accomplishment.

When you take your eyes off your goal of living a life of excellence, you will produce the mediocrity you are focusing on. This principle is illustrated in Genesis 30, which relates the time Jacob worked for his uncle Laban.

Jacob took the best goats and the best sheep and had them mate in front of branches that he had peeled to make them streaked. The animals that mated in front of these poles eventually produced spotted or streaked offspring. God shows us through this account that whatever we focus on is the very thing that will determine the outcome of our lives.

That's why I say one of the greatest enemies to your life is broken focus. For instance, suppose one day you decide you're going to start getting up early in the morning to pray. So you get up and decide to make yourself a cup of coffee first. All of a sudden, you hear one of your kids yelling for you to come help him with something. You run to take care of that situation, thinking, *Jesus, I'm coming. I'll be there in a minute.* Then the phone rings, and that conversation takes another fifteen minutes. Soon the morning is half gone, and you have to leave for a scheduled appointment.

This type of situation happens again and again in many arenas of life. A day turns into a week; a week turns into a month; and a month turns into a year. All of a sudden, you look back at your life and think, *What a fool I've been! I concentrated on things I never should have bothered with — all because of broken focus.*

Therefore, to be an excellent minister, you must learn to lock in on a goal that God gives you; then you must refuse to be distracted from pursuing that goal until you achieve it. Following this principle will bring you a tremendous amount of joy because it sets you on a sure path to excellence.

AN EXCELLENT MINISTER CANNOT DETERMINE
THE TIME OF HIS PROMOTION,
BUT HE *CAN* PREPARE HIMSELF
FOR HIS RECEPTION OF IT.

Always remember that you are in a preparation process to ready yourself for reception of all you need for the next step in God's plan for you.

Many who are called to the ministry fail in the years of preparation because they don't prepare themselves to receive the mantle God has for them. Only when they think God is close to giving them that mantle for ministry do they start scrambling to get ready — but by then it's too late.

We can see that Elisha knew the importance of readying himself for reception in Second Kings 2. When it was time for Elijah to take a journey to the place where he was to be taken up into Heaven, the older prophet did everything possible to leave Elisha behind and go alone. But Elisha said, "No! As the Lord lives and as you live, you'll never get rid of me" (v. 2).

In each city where Elijah and Elisha stopped on their journey, the sons of the prophets came out to meet them. Who were these sons of the prophets? They were men who at one time had served in the ministry; yet at some point they had gotten off the Holy Spirit's "potter's wheel." Before they were ready to receive the mantle that was on the life of

Elijah, they went off on their own to a school for prophets. They actually thought they were doing what they were supposed to be doing. Yet because they hadn't properly readied themselves, none of them had ever qualified for the mantle of the prophet of God.

Only Elisha readied himself for reception, refusing to leave his assigned place at Elijah's side until the moment had come to receive the mantle of the man of God. Then Elijah was taken up in the whirlwind, and Elisha tore off his robe as he cried, "Where is the Lord God of Elijah?" In other words, Elisha exchanged his clothes for the clothes of his spiritual father.

Notice that Elisha didn't say, "Where is *my* God?" Nor did he say, "It's time for my ministry to come forth!" He said, "Where is the Lord God of Elijah?" because he had prepared himself to receive the mantle of the prophet who had trained him in the ministry. When the moment of reception came, Elisha was ready. Immediately he ripped off his own mantle and put on the mantle of Elijah.

In the same way, you must faithfully stay by the side of the ministers to whom God assigns you, even during the difficult moments. Determine to serve these true ministers of God so you may be ready to receive the mantle the Holy Spirit has for you when the moment arrives.

Always remember that with the call to ministry comes a required qualification for the mantle — the anointing and the spiritual equipment — of that divine call. You can't obtain that mantle just because you say you want it. You can't have it just because you sat at the feet of a man of God and served him in the ministry. You have to diligently prepare yourself to receive what you need to fulfill God's call on your life.

Remember — you never know when you are only one piece of information away from putting the puzzle together that will set you on course to your God-ordained destiny. You might not be able to determine the moment a mantle is given to you, but you *can* ready yourself for reception!

AN EXCELLENT MINISTER UNDERSTANDS THAT PROMOTION COMES FROM GOD, BUT ITS TIMING IS IN THE HANDS OF MEN.

Given the principle we've just discussed, it becomes easier to understand why you can put off your future promotion by not being ready for it. The timing of that promotion will only come as you continually bow your knees, humbling yourself before God in prayer and fasting. You must also diligently meditate on the Word of God, allowing the Word to roll through your heart, your mind, your body — through every aspect of your life.

It's a matter of learning how to touch the heart of God in prayer instead of just going through some form of religious ritual. As you develop a new level of intimacy with the Holy Spirit, He will teach you not only how to receive your promotion, but also how to shorten your time between the promotions that are to come.

Timing is important for every aspect of preparing for what God has planned for your future. In fact, how you perceive what I'm telling you right now is actually setting the future seasons of your life. If you throw down this book feeling angry about what I've said, you have just set seasons of pain in your future. But the moment you read these pages and think, *You know what? I'm going to change the way I live!* you have chosen seasons of blessings for your future as you launch out to fulfill the call of God!

PRINCIPLES TO PREPARE FOR THE CALL

★ **An excellent minister understands that God has already scheduled his moment for separation unto the call, but he must ready himself for that moment.**

★ **An excellent minister pursues the change that will prepare him for the future.**

★ **An excellent minister chooses to dismantle his life in times when he can withstand the pain of change.**

★ **An excellent minister embraces short-term denial in order to create long-term benefits.**

★ **An excellent minister understands that lasting change requires rooting out yesterday's pain in order to experience relief from yesterday's memories.**

★ An excellent minister always builds his life on a firm foundation.

★ An excellent minister lives life by his principles, not by his emotions.

★ An excellent minister knows that testing is required for promotion.

★ An excellent minister knows that today's excellence is tomorrow's mediocrity.

★ An excellent minister is convinced that every step away from temptation is one step closer to God's dream within him.

★ An excellent minister knows that obedience to the known will of God is the key to unlocking His unknown will.

★ An excellent minister establishes God's principles in his life one step at a time.

★ An excellent minister uses focus to deliver him to his God-given destination.

★ An excellent minister cannot determine the time of his promotion, but he *can* prepare himself for his reception of it.

★ An excellent minister understands that promotion comes from God, but its timing is in the hands of men.

NOTES:

_____

_____

_____

_____

_____

_____

_____

_____

_____

_____

_____

_____

_____

_____

_____

_____

_____

_____

_____

_____

NOTES:

_____

_____

_____

_____

_____

_____

_____

_____

_____

_____

_____

_____

_____

_____

_____

_____

_____

_____

_____

_____

FULFILLING YOUR CALL WITH EXCELLENCE

You've been faithful in the time of preparation. Finally, the day comes when God tells you to step out in faith to fulfill your call to the ministry. Before you do, here's two questions I want you to ponder: 1) What is it you want to achieve in life? 2) *Are you willing to pay the price to achieve it?*

So many people want great things to happen to them in life, but they are unwilling to pay the price to obtain those great things. Others set overly lofty goals for themselves that they have absolutely no way of realizing.

How can you keep yourself from joining the ranks of these defeated people? The following principles of ministerial excellence provide part of the answer. Follow these principles diligently, and you will avoid becoming one of the many casualties of failed ministries that lie along the wayside of Christendom.

An excellent minister always sets goals that he is willing to wake up with a passion for every morning.

Every morning I need to wake up with the idea that I am going to be a better pastor than I was yesterday. I have to wake up with the thought, *Today I will hear the voice of Heaven with greater accuracy than ever before. I will help people experience a greater measure of freedom in their lives as they move one step closer to excellence.*

Every day I have to understand what it is going to take to make me better. I don't ever want to just "get through the day" so I can reach tomorrow. I want to be better at the end of the day than I was at the beginning.

Why do I want that? Well, it's true that man inherently has a drive on the inside of him to become greater, to multiply, to achieve goals never achieved by those who came before him. However, I know that this inner drive will never be satisfied if I just sit around and wait for "the big break." I will only satisfy the desire to excel that burns on the inside of me by pursuing what I want to possess with a full understanding of why I want to possess it.

In order to see the goal you want to achieve, you have to know why you believe what you believe. Otherwise, your pursuit of excellence in life and ministry is nothing more than wasted time.

Don't let yourself pursue something you can't achieve. Refuse to play a mental game that in the end accomplishes nothing of eternal value. Wake up tomorrow and every day thereafter with these thoughts first and foremost on your mind:

- *How can I pick up an attribute today that causes me to be more like my Heavenly Father?*

- *How am I going to use my words, my determination, and my direction to achieve what God has for me in the ministry?*

- *What can I add to my life today that will make me a better minister than I was yesterday and bring increased benefit to others?*

**AN EXCELLENT MINISTER PURSUES
THE FINISH LINE WITH AS MUCH PASSION
AS HE PURSUES THE STARTING BLOCK.**

Life is full of starters, but there are only a few finishers. Everyone looks wonderful at the starting line. But it isn't how a person starts a race that really matters in life; it's how he finishes it. Diplomas aren't handed out on registration day!

Everyone starts his or her spiritual race with the intention to win, but far too few actually come away from the race with a trophy.

That's why you need to study more about finishing than you do about starting as you step out to fulfill your call to the ministry. A transformation of affection will take place as you diligently run your race. No longer will you be looking only at the prize set before you; it will be enough that you are fighting the fight of faith in order to finish your course for the Lord.

Consider the beginning of the apostle Paul's walk with the Lord. The Bible tells us that he actually had to be led to someone's home in Damascus because he was blind and could not see. Yet we find Paul saying these words to Timothy near the end of his life:

I have fought the good fight, I have finished the race, I have kept the faith.
Finally, there is laid up for me the crown of righteousness, which the Lord, the righteous Judge, will give to me on that Day, and not to me only but also to all who have loved His appearing.

2 Timothy 4:7,8

The crown of righteousness Paul refers to here is the victor's crown. He had made it to the end of the race God had set before him in victory. It didn't matter how he started that race; it only mattered how he finished it.

So determine from the very outset that you are going to finish your course better and stronger than when you began it. Yes, you will encounter obstacles along the way. But just keep reminding yourself that it is how you finish the race that matters the most — and you will be one of those who wears the victor's crown!

> **AN EXCELLENT MINISTER ONLY KNOWS ONE PATH TO FOLLOW — THE HIGHEST ONE.**

The high road is the road God desires for you to take in every situation you encounter. You see, my friend, you may think that the devil is your greatest enemy. But the truth is, mediocrity — settling for something less than God's best — is a greater enemy. That's why you have to determine that you will always stretch for the high road not only in ministry, but in every area of your life.

One of the greatest problems in the Church today is that so many ministers live in mediocrity; yet God has called them to take the people for whom they are responsible to a higher level.

As ministers, we are to show other believers how to live. We are to believe God for better things in our lives so others can have better things in *their* lives. We have been given a divine mandate to help people eliminate the "just good enough" attitude from their lives — the attitude that says, *What I'm doing with my life is good enough. Everything's fine; I don't need to change.*

No, your life *isn't* good enough. Just ask yourself this question, and you'll see what I mean: *Is the life*

I'm presently living bringing glory to the Lord to the extent that He desires?

That's why I press for a better life every day. The excellence I am living today just isn't good enough for me. I want to give Jesus a better offering of myself tomorrow.

In Philippians 3:14, Paul tells us that we are to press toward the mark for the prize of the high calling — the upward calling that is in union with Christ Jesus. God didn't put us on this earth to waste our time pressing for petty, natural things that have no lasting value. He wants us to continually press toward a higher level — toward a life of greater excellence in Him.

Excellence is a quality residing on the inside of you that continues to reach, to press, to move on, regardless of outward circumstances. No matter what level of excellence you have attained, there is always a higher level to reach for. You can always become better tomorrow than you are today.

That applies not only to your personal life, but to your ministry as well. "That's the way we've always done it" doesn't work in the Kingdom of God. Nothing should ever stay the same except the truth of God's Word. You and those who work with you must embrace change as you constantly strive for a higher level of excellence. This is the only way to keep your ministry from becoming stale, outdated, and ineffective.

> **AN EXCELLENT MINISTER LIVES HIS LIFE**
> **WITH THE KNOWLEDGE THAT HEAVEN**
> **IS THE ONLY AUDIENCE**
> **HE IS RESPONSIBLE TO PLEASE.**

You have to live your life as Moses and not as Aaron. You see, Aaron represented the people to God, but he made the mistake of attempting to please the people instead of God. That's why Aaron yielded to the Israelites' demands and offered the golden calf to the Lord rather than offering the sacrifice *God* had instructed him to offer as a representative of the people.

On the other hand, Moses represented God to the people. Moses continually postured himself according to what the Lord wanted. In other words, Moses lived life with Heaven as his only audience; therefore, God granted him intimate access to His Presence, even speaking to him face to face (Exod. 33:11).

God is the only One you need to please because He is the only One in all the universe who truly knows what He wants; therefore, He is able to show you exactly what He wants for *your* life. People will tell you what they want you to do, but they don't really know. All they know is what they want at any given moment.

Remember — Heaven is always your audience. Other people may never see what you do in private, but Heaven is watching you all the time, no matter where you are or what time of day it is. So live each day with one primary goal in mind: to please the Father in everything you say, think, and do.

AN EXCELLENT MINISTER EMBRACES THE WORD OF GOD AS HEAVEN'S ONLY HANDBOOK ON EXCELLENCE.

The Word must take first place in your life. You must never see it as anything but your first priority.

Whatever another person says, suggests, or wants you to do must never take precedence over the Word of God, for the Word is the foundation of your entire life.

The following two passages of Scripture tell you the exact role God wants His Word to have in your life. If you'll obey these scriptures and give the Word first place, you'll find yourself prospering in every aspect of life:

> **The law of the Lord is perfect, converting the soul; the testimony of the Lord is sure, making wise the simple;**
> **The statutes of the Lord are right, rejoicing the heart; the commandment of the Lord is pure, enlightening the eyes;**
> **The fear of the Lord is clean, enduring forever; the judgments of the Lord are true and righteous altogether.**

More to be desired are they than gold, yea, than much fine gold; sweeter also than honey and the honeycomb.

Moreover by them Your servant is warned, and in keeping them there is great reward.

Who can understand his errors? Cleanse me from secret faults.

Keep back Your servant also from presumptuous sins; let them not have dominion over me. Then I shall be blameless, and I shall be innocent of great transgression.

Let the words of my mouth and the meditation of my heart be acceptable in Your sight, O Lord, my strength and my Redeemer.

Psalm 19:7-14

My son, give attention to my words; incline your ear to my sayings.

Do not let them depart from your eyes; keep them in the midst of your heart;

For they are life to those who find them, and health to all their flesh.

Proverbs 4:20-22

This world we live in is subject to God's universal laws, which are found in His Word. For instance, we don't even have to be Christians to operate in the law of sowing and reaping.

That means you are subject to God's laws as well. If you try to operate outside those laws in any area of life, you will meet with nothing but failure and defeat. Therefore, always keep this in mind: *You must never attempt to make a decision without finding the precedent in the Book to make it come to pass.*

Why is this principle so important to follow? Well, look at what happened to King Saul when he violated God's instructions.

You probably remember the story. Saul actually had a great beginning before the Lord. He wouldn't even come before the prophet of God without an offering. He was humble and small in his own eyes.

But then Saul was anointed king, and something began to change within him. Pride and rebellion began to take him down a path that eventually led to great loss and destruction. Saul made the mistake that so many of us commit. He became a people-pleaser. He thought that by being pleasing to the people, he was pleasing God.

We find the account of Saul's fatal mistake in First Samuel 15. God told Saul to lead the Israelite army in the utter destruction of the Amalekites (v. 3). Saul obeyed the Lord only in part, yielding to pressure from his people to spare the Amalekite king and the best of the Amalekite livestock.

So God woke up the prophet Samuel and said, **"I greatly regret that I have set up Saul as king, for he has turned back from following Me, and has not performed My commandments..."** (v. 11).

Samuel cried about Saul all night long because the king had disappointed God through disobedience. The next day, the prophet went to see Saul. Saul immediately walked up to Samuel and said, "Hello, Samuel. I have obeyed the voice of the Lord your God."

"Then what is the bleating of the sheep that I hear?" Samuel asked.

"Oh, that? That isn't anything."

"Yes, it is. It is evidence that you did *not* obey God. You did what you wanted to do, not what you were asked to do."

What a harsh indictment to have leveled against you for eternity! Imagine what it would be like to spend your life traveling all over the world for the sake of the Gospel, doing all kinds of wonderful works — only to come before the Judgment Seat of Christ and watch your good works burn up because you didn't do something God wanted you to do. I don't know about you, but for some reason that just wouldn't bless me very much!

Yet a multitude of Christians will go through that exact experience one day when they stand before Jesus. Why? Because they never bothered to do what God asked them to do with their lives.

That's why I use God's Word as my definitive handbook on excellence. I'm interested in what God wants, not what I want. I tell God all the time, "Lord, just tell me what You want me to do. Then I'll change *me* instead of me trying to change *You!*"

> **AN EXCELLENT MINISTER REFUSES
> TO ALLOW ANYTHING TO DETER HIM
> FROM HIS TIME ALONE WITH GOD.**

When it's time to draw away and worship God, never let anything else get in the way of that all-important priority. All the world needs to just wait until after you have worshiped the Lord, for there is nothing more important in life than spending time with the King of kings.

The truth is, the time you have spent in the past worshiping and fellowshipping with God is the primary reason you have come this far. Your private time with Him will also be what keeps you moving forward, all the way to God's upward calling in Christ Jesus.

And let me say this about your private devotional time with the Lord: You should *delight* in worshiping God. Don't just do it out of a sense of duty. As Psalm 37:4,5 (*KJV*) says:

> **Delight thyself also in the Lord; and he shall give thee the desires of thine heart.**
> **Commit thy way unto the Lord; trust also in him; and he shall bring it to pass.**

Always be willing to worship the Lord with all your heart. Be the one who worships Him in a way that is unheard of by your peers.

Remember, you're not only worshiping God because you love and adore Him and want to glorify His Name; you're also worshiping Him as an example before the people of God. That's why people need to see you freely worshiping the Lord in corporate worship. You never want them to get the idea that you avoid the worship service because you think you're too good to worship God at church.

Make it your highest priority to press into God with all your heart and your mind — with everything that you are. Be passionate about pursuing the things of God and His plans for your life. Above all, let your delight in worshiping the Lord push everything else out of the way when it's time to draw away and fellowship with Him.

> AN EXCELLENT MINISTER FOCUSES
> ON HIS ACTIONS, NOT ON HIS INTENTIONS.

If you truly want to know how well you are doing at pursuing your call to the ministry, examine what you have done, not what you have intended to do. What are the tasks you have finished, the goals you have already achieved? I'm not talking about the things you have started and only *wanted* to finish. I'm talking about the ministerial goals you have set for yourself about which you can say, "That is something I actually accomplished."

When you are in the middle of a task or in pursuit of a particular goal, don't let yourself start complaining, "Oh, this is too hard! It's just so difficult to do all that has to be done!" If you're not careful, you'll talk yourself into giving up — and then there will be one more item on your "Things Started But Never Finished" chart!

You know, God never asked you to do one easy thing yet. That's why He is pleased by faith! The day you think God has asked you to do something easy is the day you'll know it wasn't God who asked you to do it. God always asks you to do something by faith. He never asks you to do something you are able to accomplish in your own ability.

So focus on those goals you have actually achieved through Him. Remember, the road to destruction is paved with good intentions.

No one ever intended to go to hell. A person almost always believes that, when he dies, he is going to Heaven. The question is, what has that person accomplished in life? Has he accomplished that which God requires of him to be saved, or has he only intended to do what is right?

If a person will focus on what he has accomplished in the spiritual realm, he can then understand the direction his eternity is going. In the same way, if you focus on the actions you've taken to pursue excellence, you will then be able to see the direction your life and ministry is going.

AN EXCELLENT MINISTER IS ONLY INTERESTED
IN ANSWERING ONE QUESTION:
"WHAT DOES THE WORD HAVE TO SAY
ABOUT THIS SITUATION?"

This is the question to ask regarding everything that comes at you in life. What does God say about your situation? What does the Word tell you to do about it?

What God has to say is really all I'm interested in. Whatever God says about a situation, that is what I'm going to do. Whatever God believes, that's what I believe.

I can recall times in years gone by when people asked me, "How are you doing, Robb?" and I would respond, "Well, let me see." Then I would open my little Bible and say, "I can do all things through Christ which strengthens me!"

You see, I really do believe the Word of God. I don't believe my feelings. I'm not moved by what I see; I'm not moved by what I feel. I'm only moved by what I believe, and I believe what God believes!

AN EXCELLENT MINISTER CONSISTENTLY LIVES A LIFE OF HUMILITY, TREATING OTHERS AS MORE VALUABLE THAN HIMSELF.

A person who lives a life of servanthood is one who continually sees other people as better than he is and therefore treats them as such. He is a servant in the true sense of the word.

I want to give you an insight into servanthood. When many people agree to serve, they are actually serving themselves more than they are serving others.

But the test of a true servant is this: *Does a person continue to act like one when he is treated like one?*

A servant whose motives are right — who isn't just serving to gain recognition — will act like a servant even when he is treated like a servant. On the other hand, if a person gets offended when he is corrected by his superior and responds with a belligerent "who-do-you-think-you-are?" attitude, that person is *not* a true servant.

Here is another scenario that can reveal a person who is not a true servant: When an offense comes, does the person take the bait? A person who is not a true servant will just turn and walk away — still infected with that offense, even though he might not know it.

In Mark 10:35-45, James and John asked Jesus to allow them to sit at His right and His left hand when He came into His glory in Heaven. But Jesus responded with a key principle of God's Kingdom: **"...Whosoever of you will be the chiefest, shall be servant of all"** (v. 44 *KJV*).

If you choose as a minister of the Gospel to always take the place of servanthood, God will always exalt you. Why? Because the only way up with God is *down!*

Jesus also related a parable in this passage of a man who attended a wedding feast. Once there, this man decided to take the seat reserved for someone else who was very special to the governor of the feast. Now, it is possible that this man deserved such a seat of honor. But when he chose that seat for himself, the governor immediately asked him to sit in a lesser seat.

Then Jesus made the point that we are not to exalt ourselves as this man did at the wedding feast. Instead, we must choose the lower place as a reflection of our willingness to posture ourselves as a servant to others.

This is a very important principle we have to understand if we are to truly serve in the Kingdom of God. We must serve with no other motive than to be a servant, remembering that Jesus said the greatest among us will be the servant of all.

In every relationship in your life — at home, on your job, in the church, in your interactions within the Body of Christ — you can choose to be the servant. As you make that choice from your heart, God can then exalt you. Luke 14:11 says it this way: **"For whoever exalts himself will be humbled, and he who humbles himself will be exalted."**

In James 4:10, the Bible tells you that you are to humble yourself in the sight of the Lord, and He will lift you up. On the other hand, verse 6 says, **"...God resists the proud, but gives grace to the humble."** God resists the person who raises *himself* up.

It's one thing to have other people resisting you. But when *God* resists you, that's too much for anyone to bear! It's just a whole lot better to humble yourself before God and to live in continual humility as a true servant in His Kingdom!

Now, it's important to understand that repentance before man is an everyday occurrence, because repentance is a requirement every time you do something wrong to another person.

When I've wronged another person, I am more than willing to ask that person to forgive me. Whenever I need to, I'm ready to say, "Please forgive me for the way I've treated you." Then I continue in that same repentant attitude with that person for a long time to come.

If you're not willing to admit your wrongdoing and to ask forgiveness of the one you have offended or hurt, you will become arrogant and unapproachable. That's why you must live in continual repentance as a servant of others — because repentance before God may be a one-time issue, but repentance before man is an everyday occurrence.

AN EXCELLENT MINISTER UNDERSTANDS THAT THE SEEDS HE SOWS TODAY ARE THE HARVESTS HE WILL REAP IN HIS TOMORROWS.

In order for you to rise from your present level to the level God wants to take you as a minister of the Gospel, you must use *the power of the seed*. You are setting your future seasons by the seed you sow today.

Your entire life must become a seed planted in the lives of others to bring forth a harvest of salvation, healing, and deliverance in every area of life.

Only as you deliberately plant yourself as a seed in the land where you minister will you begin to bear fruit for God's Kingdom in that land.

We can see throughout the Scriptures that people often used the power of the seed in order to receive the harvest they so greatly desired. For instance, in Acts 10:1-6, we see this principle operating in the life of the Roman centurion named Cornelius.

As Cornelius prayed during the hour of prayer, the angel of the Lord appeared to him and said, "Cornelius, your prayers and your giving have come up as a memorial before God. Now send men from Joppa to a man whose name is Peter. He will tell you what you must do" (vv. 4-6).

Can you imagine that type of salutation? God recognized a person because of his giving! That speaks volumes about the power of the seed!

Now, it is possible that Cornelius was the same centurion talked about in Luke 7:2-9, who asked Jesus to come heal his servant. Look at the reason the Pharisees gave Jesus that this particular centurion was worthy to have his request fulfilled: **"For he loves our nation, and has built us a synagogue"** (v. 5).

How did the Pharisees know that this centurion loved the people of God? Because he had built them a synagogue. Giving is such positive proof of a person's love!

Now let me ask you two very simple but direct questions: How do other people know how much you love them? How does God know how much you love Him and how much you want to be everything He wants you to be? *By the seed you sow to bring forth a better life* — not only for yourself, but also for all those with whom you come in contact.

AN EXCELLENT MINISTER USES THE POWER LOCKED UP IN THE SEED TO EMBRACE GOD'S FUTURE ASSIGNMENT.

Everything in our lives requires a seed. That's why we see so many instances in the Word of God where people use the power of the seed in order to create a future.

After King David went home to be with the Lord and his son, Solomon, became king, the Bible tells us that Solomon offered a thousand burnt offerings to the Lord on the altar of God. That same night, God appeared to him and asked, "What can I do for you?" (2 Chron. 1:7-12).

Think about that. Here was a man who had just been given the job of governing the greatest kingdom on the face of the earth. As a servant of the true and the living God, Solomon realized he needed to plant seed in the ground in order to bring forth the harvest of provision he needed to fulfill that great responsibility.

The power of that seed produced results before even one day had passed! That very night, God appeared to him and asked, "What can I do for you?"

Solomon answered, **"Now give me wisdom and knowledge, that I may go out and come in before this people; for who can judge this great people of Yours?"** (v. 10).

God liked Solomon's humble answer. Verses 11 and 12 give His response:

Then God said to Solomon: "Because this was in your heart, and you have not asked riches or wealth or honor or the life of your enemies, nor have you asked long life — but have asked wisdom and knowledge for yourself, that you may judge My people over whom I have made you king —

"wisdom and knowledge are granted to you; and I will give you riches and wealth and honor, such as none of the kings have had who were before you, nor shall any after you have the like."

Don't hesitate to follow Solomon's example. You get God's attention when you plant seed in the ground in anticipation of *your* future harvest!

You can also go to the New Testament to find those who got God's attention because of the seed they sowed. For instance, Mark 12:41-44 tells the story of the widow who only put two cents in the offering. But Jesus took notice of that woman's offering; in fact, He said she put in more than everyone else!

Why did Jesus say that? *Because the value of a seed is not determined by how much you sow, but by how much it cost you to sow it.*

Then in Acts 4:36 and 37 (*NIV*), we are introduced to a sower named Joseph.

> **Joseph, a Levite from Cyprus, whom the apostles called Barnabas (which means Son of Encouragement),**
> **sold a field he owned and brought the money and put it at the apostles' feet.**

The apostles changed Joseph's name to Barnabus, or "the Son of Encouragement." Why did the apostles do that? Because of the seed Barnabus had sown. He was noticed by what he gave.

In Acts 9:36-38 we see a woman named Tabitha, or Dorcas, who created her future by continuing to sow and sow and sow into the lives of others. When she died, those who loved her went to get Peter. When he came to where Dorcas lay, they showed Peter all the garments she had made for people in need. When Peter saw all the gifts Dorcas had given to help others, he told everyone to leave the room; then he knelt down beside her bedside to pray. Within moments, Dorcas had been raised from the dead by the power of God because of the seed she had sown!

So never underestimate the power of the seed to produce a harvest of blessing for your tomorrows. As you live the lifestyle of a giver, your seed will rise up before God in remembrance, and He will move on your behalf to produce the harvest you need to fulfill your call in excellence!

> **AN EXCELLENT MINISTER KNOWS THAT
> AT TIMES HE MUST BEGIN THE FLOW OF GIVING
> IN ORDER TO RELEASE OTHERS
> INTO THE ABUNDANCE OF GOD.**

As we saw in Acts 4:36 and 37, Joseph (later called Barnabus) started the giving. He was already a ministry-minded person, even at the beginning of the infant Church.

God often uses a minister of excellence to open the flow of giving. Many times the Lord has instructed me to be the first person to give in a church service. Why does He do this? Because if I expect anyone else to do something, I must first be willing to do it myself.

When God uses me in this way, the speaker's exhortation to give into the work of the Lord often seems to be falling on deaf ears. Then I say, "I'll give to that ministry. I'll take care of that specific need you just mentioned." Suddenly, a flood of giving begins.

Why does it work this way? Because an excellent minister knows how to release others into abundance! That's why you should never be surprised if the Lord uses you to give generously at the beginning of a new ministry project.

Many people have the perception that ministers are professional receivers but paupers when it comes to sowing. As a minister of excellence, you must turn that perception around by becoming a professional sower.

I like to say it like this: Every business has a shipping department and a receiving department. I asked God long ago if I could work in His shipping department. Meanwhile, I know He will always make sure I have things coming to me from the receiving department!

> **An excellent minister realizes the road to abundance is paved by living a balanced life.**

Don't ever let yourself stand out ostentatiously so that you overshadow others in the environment where you minister. Instead, understand the environment you must walk in, and stay balanced in the way you live there. Remember, **"a false balance is abomination to the Lord: but a just weight is his delight"** (Prov. 11:1 *KJV*).

You have to stay balanced in every area as you build your life and ministry on a foundation of excellence. Never attempt to live on the outside what you are not already living on the inside.

I remember an incident in my life that illustrates this principle. A car dealer who wanted to bless me once offered to sell me a very valuable automobile for the same price as the much less valuable car that I was in the process of purchasing. I told the manager I had to think about his offer for a little while.

A couple of days went by before I finally responded to the car dealer. When I did, I said to him, "Thank you for your offer, but I must decline at this time."

The salesman asked, "Why would you do that? This car is worth so much less than the one I'm offering you for the same price. Why would you want the one that is so much less valuable? We're willing to almost give away this more expensive car to you!"

I replied, "Because I don't fit in this automobile yet. It isn't my time to be there. I never want to try to be something on the outside that I am not already on the inside."

So maintain a balance in every aspect of your life, and stretch for the high road in every situation. Live the life of a true servant and a professional sower. Focus on your actions, not your intentions, and finish every assignment you begin. It's all part of being an excellent minister as you fulfill the call of God on your life!

PRINCIPLES FOR FULFILLING THE CALL

★ **An excellent minister always sets goals that he is willing to wake up with a passion for every morning.**

★ **An excellent minister pursues the finish line with as much passion as he pursues the starting block.**

★ **An excellent minister only knows one path to follow — the highest one.**

★ An excellent minister lives his life with the knowledge that Heaven is the only audience he is responsible to please.

★ An excellent minister embraces the Word of God as Heaven's only handbook on excellence.

★ An excellent minister refuses to allow anything to deter him from his time alone with God.

★ An excellent minister focuses on his actions, not on his intentions.

★ An excellent minister is only interested in answering one question: "What does the Word have to say about this situation?"

★ An excellent minister consistently lives a life of humility, treating others as more valuable than himself.

★ An excellent minister understands that the seeds he sows today are the harvests he will reap in his tomorrows.

★ An excellent minister uses the power locked up in the seed to embrace God's future assignment.

★ An excellent minister knows that at times he must begin the flow of giving in order to release others into the abundance of God.

★ **An excellent minister realizes the road to abundance is paved by living a balanced life.**

NOTES:

NOTES:

_____

_____

_____

_____

_____

_____

_____

_____

_____

_____

_____

_____

_____

_____

_____

_____

_____

_____

_____

_____

RELATING TO AUTHORITY WITH EXCELLENCE

As a minister, your entire life is centered around relating to other people. Therefore, an important key to establishing a ministry of excellence is understanding your scriptural role in all your different relationships. To that end, I'm going to share some principles in these next few chapters that will help you relate with excellence to those whom God has placed in your life.

AN EXCELLENT MINISTER ASSESSES WHO AND WHAT HE IS IN EVERY RELATIONSHIP AND THEN POSTURES HIMSELF ACCORDINGLY.

As a minister, one of the most important aspects in this arena of relationships is the way you posture yourself when you are with other people. Whenever you are in a relationship with another person, you must continually assess who God wants you to be in that relationship.

It's very important to me that I put myself in the position God wants me to assume in any given relationship. I never assume a position or a role that God hasn't given to me. I recognize who I am in my God-assigned position, and I embrace that position. I'm very happy to be there.

For instance, I have the privilege of knowing some great men of God, but I don't try to be a spiritual mentor to them. I'm not out to push what I know on them. Should they discover it, it will be their treasure. But until that day, I posture myself where I'm supposed to be in my relationship with each of them — in the role of servant to a greater man of God — and immediately seek to become significant in that person's life.

If the person is my peer and my equal, I still choose to assume the role of a servant, even though I recognize that he is my equal and that we fellowship horizontally. However, rather than serving my equal in the same way I serve the greater man of God, I serve him with my love, my openness, and my fellowship.

Finally, there are those God has placed under my authority. I am called to speak into the lives of these people. I tell them the things God wants me to tell them. I posture myself as one who speaks to them regarding the things of God. I am a person they are pursuing in order to receive the information for life that God wants them to have.

You, too, have a position in each relationship you have with other people. Whether the person is over you, your equal, or under your authority, you must assess and embrace your position to which God has assigned you. Recognize who you are and, even more, who you are *not* in that relationship — and then act accordingly.

> ## AN EXCELLENT MINISTER DOESN'T TRY TO IMPRESS EVERYONE BUT WORKS DILIGENTLY TO IMPRESS A SPECIAL FEW.

You cannot be effective in the ministry if you spread yourself too thin in the arena of relationships. You only have so much love, so much seed, and so much time. That's why you can only be exclusive with a few. So instead of trying to develop a lot of intimate relationships with people, start whittling unnecessary relationships out of your life. Otherwise, you will waste time sowing seed into the lives of people God never intended for you to be close to.

If you concentrate on those whom God has placed in your life, your life will continually move upward. But if you allow the wrong people to be in your environment, your life will begin to descend in a continual downward spiral. As Proverbs 13:20 says so clearly, **"He who walks with wise men will be wise, but the companion of fools will be destroyed."**

This is why I don't try to impress everyone; I focus on those who can have the greatest impact on me, as well as those I can have the greatest impact on. Why? Because an excellent minister strives to be someone who is good to all but excellent to a special few!

Now I want to share some important principles to apply to your relationships with the "special few" whom God has placed over you in the Lord. As you make it your aim to bring benefit to these people in your life, I guarantee you that you will receive priceless benefits in return.

AN EXCELLENT MINISTER EMBRACES AND PROTECTS THE AUTHORITIES HE IS ASSIGNED TO.

One of the greatest things you can ever know as a minister and as a believer is that *God works through the chain of authority*. We find a number of authority structures throughout the Word of God.

First, there is the structure of the government. Romans 13:1-4 tells us the way we are to respond to our government:

> **Let every soul be subject to the governing authorities. For there is no authority except from God, and the authorities that exist are appointed by God.**
> **Therefore whoever resists the authority resists the ordinance of God, and those who resist will bring judgment on themselves.**
> **For rulers are not a terror to good works, but to evil. Do you want to be**

unafraid of the authority? Do what is good, and you will have praise from the same.

For he is God's minister to you for good. But if you do evil, be afraid; for he does not bear the sword in vain; for he is God's minister, an avenger to execute wrath on him who practices evil.

God has also established authority structures within the family (Eph. 5:22-6:4) and at the workplace (Eph. 6:5-8). Finally, there is the authority structure within the local church:

> The elders who are among you I exhort, I who am a fellow elder and a witness of the sufferings of Christ, and also a partaker of the glory that will be revealed:
> Shepherd the flock of God which is among you, serving as overseers, not by compulsion but willingly, not for dishonest gain but eagerly;
> nor as being lords over those entrusted to you, but being examples to the flock....
> Likewise you younger people, submit yourselves to your elders....

1 Peter 5:1-3,5

These are the basic authority structures God has laid out in His Word. The closer you stick to your God-ordained authorities in life, the more reward you can expect to receive.

However, the highest reward results from obeying the authority structure within the church. You see, your relationship with God is inseparably tied to a relationship with the local church. You cannot separate the two, no matter how hard you try.

God cannot reward you outside the authority structures He has established in His Word. So make it your aim to embrace and to protect your authority structure in the church. As you do, you will open the way for God to abundantly bless you.

AN EXCELLENT MINISTER IS FULLY AWARE THAT SOMEONE GREATER THAN HIMSELF IS MONITORING HIS EVERY MOVE TO REWARD HIM.

Recognize that there is always an unseen observer who sees you when the rest of the world is silent and Heaven doesn't seem to hear your prayers. Someone is always noticing you even when no one else is looking.

The person who is over you in the Lord is looking over your shoulder. He is there to help you prepare, to help you focus, and to help you understand the future God has for you. When it looks like the world is pushing you away and God has no future for you, the person God has placed over you will always be there to encourage and to love you.

AN EXCELLENT MINISTER WELCOMES INSTRUCTION.

There has to be someone in your life whom you trust enough to confront you with the need for change. Genesis 18 relates a situation with Sarah that illustrates this principle. The Lord came to visit Abraham along with two angels. God was about to destroy Sodom and Gomorrah, but He said, "I can't do this without talking to my man Abraham, because part of his family is living in Sodom."

During the Lord's visit at Abraham's home, He told Abraham that Sarah was going to bear a son (Gen. 18:10-15). Verse 15 tells us Sarah's response to the Lord's message to Abraham: *she laughed.*

When the Lord confronted Sarah about her laughing, she denied that she had done it. The Lord just replied, "No, but you did laugh."

That's what you must have in your life — someone in your life you trust enough to tell you that you laughed even when you don't think you did!

In other words, you must learn to take down your guard and receive correction when someone you trust dearly comes to you and tells you that you have done something wrong. As Proverbs 9:9 says, **"Give instruction to a wise man, and he will be still wiser; teach a just man, and he will increase in learning."**

Be willing to accept an ever greater measure of examination from your superiors who are close to you. Remember, the people in your life who care about you the most are usually the toughest on you. Why? Because they have committed themselves to you for your benefit, to help you fulfill God's call on your life. They're willing to pay the price to get beyond your flesh and help you change for the better.

You can't please everyone in your life, so don't try. Never waste your time taking instructions from someone who cannot promote you. Focus instead on pleasing those over you in the Lord who can give you a promotion — the people who can speak a word and change your life forever!

AN EXCELLENT MINISTER ENGAGES ONLY WITH THOSE FOR WHOM HE HAS PREPARED.

If I'm not ready to approach an individual to whom God has assigned me, I simply don't approach him. "But what if that time never comes?" you may ask. Then I've passed up my opportunity because I didn't properly prepare myself.

One of the most important aspects of preparing yourself to approach someone over you in the Lord is to make sure you have a good attitude. I'm sure you can think of a time in your life when your own bad attitude cost you long-term consequences. That's why timing is so important when you approach someone God has placed over you in life. Make sure you're ready — and then approach!

AN EXCELLENT MINISTER SEEKS TO NETWORK WITH OTHERS OF THE SAME SPIRIT.

Excellence has to be surrounded by excellence, or it will compromise. In other words, if you're not continually associating with other people of excellence, mediocre people will continually try to pull you back to the mediocre level where you lived in the past.

That's why it's so important to network with individuals who are of the same heart and have the same inner drive for excellence as you do. The people you choose to network with largely determine how well you continue to grow and become successful in your life and ministry.

Yes, there are many types of people who hold different positions in your life. But you must never lose sight of this fact: *The people with whom you presently have close relationships will either take you up or take you down in life.* Therefore, God wants you to spend the bulk of your time with those whose lives you are *moving toward* as you follow His will for your life — not those you are *coming from.*

So surround yourself with people of your future, not with people of your past. In other words, make sure you always choose to associate closely with the people who are a part of your tomorrows, not the people who might draw you back into yesterday.

AN EXCELLENT MINISTER IS KEENLY AWARE THAT RESPECT GUARANTEES ACCESS.

Respect actually guarantees you access to the life you desire to live. You see, whatever you respect will move toward you, and whatever you disrespect will move away from you. For instance, if you respect money, money will come toward you. If you disrespect money — if you think it's unimportant or undesirable — money will move away from you.

I've had people whom God has placed over me say, "Your respect for me is inconceivable to me, Robb. I can't figure you out."

I reply, "Respectfully, Sir, you never will. I guess you'll just have to receive that respect and leave it at that." You see, respect is like love; it comes from the heart of the one who is giving it — and my heart desires to show the utmost of respect to those God has assigned me to serve.

One aspect of respect is to realize that you are never anything until someone in authority over you openly says that you are. You are not what you say you are; you are what *others* say you are. Those whom God has placed over you can more accurately define who you are because they watch what you do. As Jesus said, **"...By their fruits you will know them"** (Matt. 7:18).

You see, people's actions determine who they really are. For instance, many people walk in pride and arrogance because they think they are someone they're really not. They have even given themselves a position in life; however, that position was never bequeathed to them by those who have the authority in their lives to tell them who they really are. These prideful people are in self-deception because they have never respected those placed over them enough to receive their counsel.

> **AN EXCELLENT MINISTER KNOWS THAT HE MUST NEVER ATTEMPT TO TAKE AUTHORITY OVER SOMETHING THAT GOD HAS NOT MADE HIM RESPONSIBLE FOR.**

You must never hold on to an opinion about something for which God hasn't made you responsible.

People sometimes ask me, "Well, what do you think about that person's decision?"

I reply, "I don't think about it."

"Well, why not?"

"Because I'm not responsible for it!"

I just make it a practice to obey First Thessalonians 4:11 — I study to be quiet, and I mind my own business!

> **AN EXCELLENT MINISTER HAS LEARNED TO RECEIVE INSTRUCTION FROM CRITICISM WITHOUT BEING OFFENDED.**

As a minister, you must never get offended by anything a superior says to you. Instead, you should immediately posture yourself to receive instruction.

Many ministers aren't even willing to quietly take criticism when it's something they don't want to hear. Don't let yourself make that mistake. In fact, you have to go beyond the point of just being able to take criticism with your mouth shut. You need to press into learning how to receive instruction by asking yourself: *How do I handle this correctly? How can I be instructed regarding what this person is saying? How can I get better at what I'm doing?*

AN EXCELLENT MINISTER UNDERSTANDS THAT IMMEDIATE ATTENTION TO DETAIL WILL GET THE PROMPT ATTENTION OF THOSE WHO CAN CHANGE HIS FUTURE.

We see this principle in operation in Joseph's life. Joseph understood that his immediate attention to detail got the immediate attention of the one whom he sought to please. When he first began to work for Potiphar as a slave, he quickly excelled in every area to which he was assigned. At that point, Potiphar began to notice him. Joseph finally reached the highest level in Potiphar's house, for Potiphar had placed his entire household under Joseph's supervision. Why? Because he saw that everything prospered in Joseph's hand.

Just as was true with Joseph, your immediate attention to detail will continually cause you to excel in everything you put *your* hand to. That gets people's attention and guarantees promotion to the next level!

> **AN EXCELLENT MINISTER UNDERSTANDS THAT
> EVERYTHING WITHIN THE WILL OF GOD
> POSSESSES ITS OWN DEFINING MOMENT.**

Habakkuk 2:2,3 gives us a clue about the importance of timing from God's perspective:

"Then the Lord answered me and said: "Write the vision and make it plain on tablets, that he may run who reads it.

For the vision is yet for an appointed time....

God's plan for your life *will* come to pass. Don't worry about it. Don't think that God has forgotten about you or that He has left you behind, because He hasn't. God is actually preparing you for everything He has for you. As you relate in truth to those who are over you in the Lord, you will find that God's purposes *will* come to pass in your life at the appointed time.

> **AN EXCELLENT MINISTER CHOOSES TO WAKE UP
> EVERY MORNING AS A PROBLEM-SOLVER
> FOR THOSE TO WHOM HE IS ASSIGNED.**

If I'm assigned to a person's life, my entire life is continually linked up to the problems I can solve for them. I continually ask myself, *Where can I see a problem in that person's life? How can I fix that problem? What can I do to make that situation better?*

I'm so excited that God allows me to be a problem-solver in the lives of other people. It makes me happy to take that position in the lives of those God has placed over me. I'd rather be remembered for the problems I *solve* for them than for the problems I *create*!

AN EXCELLENT MINISTER GIVES HIS SUPERIOR WHAT THAT PERSON WANTS, NOT WHAT HE WANTS TO GIVE HIM.

Remember this when you desire to bring a gift to those you serve in the Lord: *The only gifts that will ever be remembered will not be the gifts you want to give someone; they will be the gifts that person wants to receive.*

Each and every person has something particular he or she wants to receive in life. Personally, I search for the things people want to receive. I don't give a person what I want to give him. I don't try to sow what I want to sow. I sow what the person will respond to.

The same is true in the natural realm with the different kinds of seeds farmers sow. A patch of farmland won't remain fertile if corn is sown in it every year for a long period of time. The farmer has to change the kind of seed he sows because every seed requires different types of nutrients. He therefore determines the kind of seed by the type of ground it will be sown into.

Similarly, I look for and study what my superior wants. Then I choose to plant the kind of seed in that person's life that he wants to receive, not just the kind I want to give him. Thus, I become significant in his life as he receives a harvest of blessing.

> **AN EXCELLENT MINISTER EVALUATES WHAT OTHERS ARE NOT AND FROM HIS HEART BECOMES WHAT IS NECESSARY.**

I believe this is one of the most essential keys that has helped set my life on the path to success. I evaluate people whenever I walk in a room and immediately begin to discern the gifts and strengths, as well as the weaknesses, of each person present. Then I focus in on people's weaknesses because my ability to help in those weak areas is what makes me significant in their lives.

You see, I am unnecessary in a person's life unless I can solve a problem for that person.

Some people look at their relationships with others and protest, "But we're not trying to solve each other's problems; we just want to hang around together."

People don't just hang around with other people for no reason. They hang around with people who solve a problem for them.

So I focus on what people *are not* rather than what they *are*. I celebrate their strengths, but I become what is weak in them because that's exactly what they need from me.

A person needs you to fill in where he is weak. He doesn't need you to help in the areas where he is strong. You actually can take the role of a mentor in another person's life when you relate to him from the point of his weakness rather than the point of his strength.

For instance, I don't sit down with the great men of God to whom I am personally assigned and try to teach them anything. I speak when I'm spoken to. If they want to know what I know, I will be glad to share it with them — but I only do it if they ask.

Understand this, my friend: *A teacher may catch the knowledge you have, but he is never to be taught by you.* He is never your student. You are never to dishonor someone who is above you by attempting to make that person your student.

At the same time, your superior is actually learning from you all the time if you're smart enough to become what he is not. Why is this? Because you're strengthening his weaknesses without even saying a word about it. Eventually he might say, "You know, I'm learning so much from you. I don't know if I can live without you."

Then you can say, "Well, I guess that's why you need me!"

You see, people don't need you for the qualities in you that are the same ones they possess. They don't invite you into their lives because of your *similarities* to them; they need you and invite you because of your *differences.*

So if you want to become significant to the person God has placed over you, discover the tasks other people have never wanted to perform for him. Just go to him and ask, "What is the job no one else wants?

"Well, why are you asking me that?"

"Because that's the job I want."

"Well, why would you want to do that? Everybody hates doing that."

"No, it's okay — I love doing it."

Asking to be assigned to those unwanted tasks will give you significance in that person's life, for you will succeed where other people have refused to go. You will get the attention of the one you seek to please just because you are willing to fulfill responsibilities other people have been unwilling to take on.

As you pursue this course of excellence, you will come to the point where you're not important to yourself any longer. Instead, Philippians 2:3 (*NIV*) will become a reality in your life:

Do nothing out of selfish ambition or vain conceit, but in humility consider others better than yourselves.

In fact, meeting the needs of the person to whom you are assigned will come to mean more to you than breathing itself!

> **AN EXCELLENT MINISTER ALWAYS MAKES IT HIS AIM TO EXCEED PEOPLE'S EXPECTATIONS.**

Everyone you encounter in life as a minister has specific expectations of you. Therefore, the only way for you to excel in the eyes of those who are over you in the Lord is to "under-promise and over-perform" — in other words, to promise less than you actually give them and to always give them more than they expect.

Every day you must choose to be better than you were yesterday in your service to the people whom God has placed over you. It isn't enough that they understand why you couldn't produce to the extent you intended to. You should be the one everyone depends on because your performance always exceeds expectations.

> **AN EXCELLENT MINISTER IS ALWAYS EAGER TO PLEASE THOSE TO WHOM GOD HAS ASSIGNED HIM.**

According to Ephesians 6:5 (*AMP*), you should choose to be pleasing to those God has assigned you to:

Servants (slaves), be obedient to those who are your physical masters, having respect for them and eager concern to

please them, in singleness of motive and with all your heart, as [service] to Christ [Himself].

Sometimes we make the mistake of thinking that we only need to please God, not other people. But Ephesians 6:5 says we must actually *pursue* being pleasing to those who are over us in authority. That's something we must deliberately choose to do. Pleasing others instead of ourselves certainly doesn't come naturally!

I choose to please my superiors. I want to please them. I never want them to say, "Gosh, I wish you'd do more!" I never want them to have to correct me about *anything*. (But if they ever do find the need to correct me, I want to be someone who receives correction without crying about it — at least until I'm all alone!)

When you seek to please those in authority over you, you are ultimately pleasing God as well. But you simply cannot please God if you are not pleasing to others.

AN EXCELLENT MINISTER NEVER TAKES HIS GOD-ORDAINED RELATIONSHIPS FOR GRANTED.

You must never allow the invitation to intimacy to be destroyed by the contempt of familiarity. In other words, never take a relationship for granted because, in doing so, you can allow a very good relationship to become an old, stale relationship. That happens when you stop esteeming your relationship with someone as a valuable treasure and you become somewhat sloppy in the way you relate to that person.

As soon as you begin to become more intimate with a person, you must work at maintaining the same level of respect and manners in the relationship that you had before. Never let the invitation to intimacy make you so familiar with someone that you no longer treat that person with respect.

The bottom line is this: *Always hold the relationships God gives you in high esteem.* Make the determination that you will never let go of them.

I will absolutely never let go of my important relationships by allowing the people in my life to become so familiar that I take them for granted. I don't ever want to lose those relationships, so I will continue to sow good seed into them every day. Because of my love for these people, I am committed for life to passionately pursue my relationships with them.

This is the commitment you must make in your relationships with the people God has placed over you in the Lord. You see, you will live in the memory of their last encounter with you. They will always remember what happened the last time you spoke to them and how they felt when they left your presence.

That's why Proverbs 11:24,25 (*NIV*) tells us that we must choose to become refreshing to those God has assigned us to:

One man gives freely, yet gains even more; another withholds unduly, but comes to poverty.

A generous man will prosper; he who refreshes others will himself be refreshed.

Personally, I've made it my goal to make my superiors feel better every time they are with me. I want them to think, *You know, I just love talking to Robb. Every time I talk to him, I'm encouraged. It's the way he looks at life that makes things different. Every time I come in contact with him, he's like a breath of fresh air!*

Let that be your goal as well, my friend. Make sure you understand where God wants you to invest your loyalties in life. Then stay diligent in your pursuit to please those who are over you in the Lord. Pay attention to detail; strive to solve their problems; and treat them with unending respect and esteem. Remember, they are monitoring your every move to reward you!

PRINCIPLES FOR
RELATING TO AUTHORITY

✶ **An excellent minister assesses who and what he is in every relationship and then postures himself accordingly.**

✶ **An excellent minister doesn't try to impress everyone but works diligently to impress a special few.**

★ An excellent minister embraces and protects the authorities he is assigned to.

★ An excellent minister is fully aware that someone greater than himself is monitoring his every move to reward him.

★ An excellent minister welcomes instruction.

★ An excellent minister engages only with those for whom he has prepared.

★ An excellent minister seeks to network with others of the same spirit.

★ An excellent minister is keenly aware that respect guarantees access.

★ An excellent minister knows that he must never attempt to take authority over something that God has not made him responsible for.

★ An excellent minister has learned to receive instruction from criticism without being offended.

★ An excellent minister understands that immediate attention to detail will get the prompt attention of those who can change his future.

★ An excellent minister understands that everything within the will of God possesses its own defining moment.

★ An excellent minister chooses to wake up every morning as a problem-solver for those to whom he is assigned.

★ An excellent minister gives his superior what that person wants, not what he wants to give him.

★ An excellent minister evaluates what others are not and from his heart becomes what is necessary.

★ An excellent minister always makes it his aim to exceed people's expectations.

★ An excellent minister is always eager to please those to whom God has assigned him.

★ An excellent minister never takes his God-ordained relationships for granted.

NOTES:

_____

_____

_____

_____

_____

_____

_____

NOTES:

ESTEEMING THE VALUE OF A SPIRITUAL FATHER

In life there are only two ways to receive wisdom and enter into the will of God. The first way is *through failure.* You can fail, get up, fail, get up, fail, get up, fail, get up — until, finally, you learn your lesson and decide to obey God and follow His plan for your life.

The problem with this first method is that you have to have enough time to overcome all the failures, and you *don't* have that time. You only have a certain number of days and a certain number of cycles to make the right decision in any given situation. Why? Because God has established consequences for sin and disobedience that will eventually come to pass in your life if you continue down that wrong path.

The second way you can receive wisdom is *through a spiritual father.* You can learn from your spiritual father's experience the easy way, or you can learn from the consequences of your mistakes the hard way. It's your choice.

The truth is, you can have no greater relationship in all the world than your relationship with a spiritual father. That's why I urge you to embrace that relationship. God gives you a spiritual father because He passes His mantles generationally. In other words, God passes His mantles down through the family structure because He has always wanted a family. Remember, God is called our Heavenly Father, and He desires for us to continue the father-son relationship down here on the earth.

One of the things I have found in my relationships with the spiritual fathers God has given me is that wisdom comes to my life as I embrace these relationships more and more. The more I embrace a father, the more his wisdom comes to me, because *wisdom is only transferred through relationship*, not through knowledge.

It's important to understand that wisdom and knowledge are two different things. Knowledge has a protective covering over it, and wisdom will not come out of that knowledge until we break into relationship. We can see this principle in the father-son relationship of Moses and Joshua: **"Now Joshua the son of Nun was full of the spirit of wisdom, for Moses had laid his hands on him..."** (Deut. 34:9).

Solomon is another example of this principle manifested in a person's life. Solomon was the one son of David who listened and followed the wisdom that his father imparted to him (at least in the earlier years of his life); therefore, Solomon was the son whom God chose to become the next king.

Many of us who have natural-born sons don't necessarily give those sons the greatest wisdom of our hearts. There may be someone outside our natural family we are more open with. It all depends on who pursues us with a desire to learn what we can teach them.

God opens my heart to that kind of son, whether or not he is natural born to me. Why? Because a son of mine in the faith embraces the wisdom of my life.

The benefits you can gain from your relationship with your spiritual father are impossible to measure, for this particular relationship is key to your success in fulfilling God's call on your life. A father's wisdom will help you get around the pitfalls and the mistakes you are likely to make without him.

If you want to test the truth of that statement, just look at the life of Rehoboam (1 Kings 12:1-17). Rehoboam was the son of King Solomon — the son who reigned as king of Israel after Solomon died. Solomon's advisors told Rehoboam that the people would serve him faithfully if he would honor and love them.

But Rehoboam didn't listen to his father's advisors. Instead, he listened to his peers, who told him, "No, that isn't what you should do. You should tell the people that if they don't do what you want them to do, you're going to make it far tougher on them than your father ever dreamed of doing."

So that's what Rehoboam did. He said to the people, "If you think my father was tough, my little finger will be thicker than my father's loins!" (1 Kings 12:10). What were the immediate results of Rehoboam's refusal to follow the wisdom of his father and of his father's advisors? The nation split down the middle and became the northern and southern kingdoms of Israel.

Later more destruction came when Egypt ransacked the treasures of God's temple (1 Kings 14:25,26). If Rehoboam had listened to his father and to his father's advisors, these tragic results would have never happened. But because Rehoboam *wouldn't* listen, destruction came upon him and his nation.

Let me make an observation from my heart at this time. There are many sons who have walked away their fathers thinking that they had received everything their fathers had to offer. But there couldn't be anything further from the truth. They may have received a *blessing*, but they never received an *inheritance*.

Our example is Elijah and Elisha. The sons of the prophets in all those towns received a blessing from Elijah, but only Elisha received the inheritance. (As you read Second Kings 2, you will see that the sons of the prophets were attempting to pull Elisha away from his inheritance as well, but he vehemently refused.)

With all this in mind, let me give you some important principles that will help you identify the spiritual father in your life so you can relate to that father as a wise son.

> **A SPIRITUAL FATHER IS NEVER**
> **A PERSON WHOSE ADVICE YOU *LOOK FOR*;**
> **HE IS A PERSON WHOSE ADVICE YOU *FOLLOW*.**

A spiritual father in my life is not someone whose opinions I listen to; he is someone whose counsel I follow. I don't question his integrity, his dignity, his motives, or his ability to make decisions.

I am very serious about my relationship with a father because I've already proven my ignorance in the past. I know I have great imperfections. I can't even imagine how difficult it is to be God and have to put up with me! Therefore, I know God has given me my father-son relationships for instruction and counsel, and I am determined to follow the wisdom I receive.

Now, I'm not the only one who needs this type of relationship. We all need a father in our lives who can show us our blind spots.

We already looked at Genesis 18, where the Bible relates the time the Lord confronted Sarah with *her* blind spot. In this passage of Scripture, the role of a father can be clearly seen.

When Sarah protested that she hadn't laughed at the thought of bearing a son, she wasn't hiding anything. She really thought she didn't laugh.

Remember, there are times in our lives when we are just like Sarah. We don't think we laughed, but we really did. These are the times we need a spiritual father to correct us and to help us see what needs to change in our lives.

In Sarah's case, it took the Lord saying, "Yes, you did laugh" to reveal Sarah's blind spot and give her correction. However, it was still up to Sarah to act on God's word regarding a future son. She still had to stand in faith until she received the manifestation of the promise.

If you ever ask your spiritual father for advice but then don't follow the advice he gives you, you have just proven that one of two things is true: 1) You shouldn't have asked the question because you didn't want the answer; or 2) that person isn't really your father.

I can tell which individuals consider me their spiritual father. These are the people who not only ask for my advice; they *follow* my advice as well. People who merely ask for my advice without possessing a serious intent to follow it are just wasting my time.

Therefore, if I notice that certain individuals continually ask me for counsel yet don't necessarily do the things I say, I know I'm not the one who is assigned to be a spiritual father in their lives. I cannot afford to just continually hand out more and more information that never produces fruit in a person's life. I don't have that kind of time to waste. Jesus said it very well in

Luke 6:46: "But why do you call Me 'Lord, Lord,' and do not do the things which I say?"

I remember the time a man of God whom I consider to be a spiritual father sat down with me and said, "You know, I believe the Lord is going to use you in this particular situation."

Immediately I stopped him and said, "Sir, forgive me for interrupting, but I want to tell you something right now. Whatever you say next will be done before the sun goes down, so please calculate what you want to say. Don't suggest, and don't hint. Tell me what you want. No matter how painful it is, I will do it before the sun goes down."

All of a sudden, the conversation entered an entirely new dimension. Why? Because most spiritual leaders who want to speak into someone's life have to "tiptoe around" what they really want to say in order to get that person to receive their counsel.

I don't want that, so I tell those who are in the position of father in my life, "Don't tiptoe with me. Don't make me guess. Just tell me the truth, and I'll act on your word."

It is so important that you esteem the counsel of your spiritual father, because life doesn't get any easier as you continue to pursue God's call. You will face new levels of difficulty that you will have to pass through victoriously in order to obtain the deeper place in God that He desires for you.

That's why you need a father to help guide you through the difficult times. When you face complex situations where there seems to be no black-and-white answer, you will be able to draw on his wisdom to help you make the right decision.

> **A SPIRITUAL FATHER IS WILLING
> TO TAKE RESPONSIBILITY
> FOR YOUR WRONGDOING — TO PAY THE PRICE
> WHEN YOU DON'T POSSESS THE CURRENCY
> THAT IS REQUIRED IN ANY GIVEN SITUATION.**

Many people will tell you what they believe your next step should be. But your spiritual father isn't just willing to give you advice; he is the one who is willing to stay with you even if you make a wrong decision. He is there to help you make it through the difficult consequences of your mistake so you can come out on the other side victoriously.

> **A SPIRITUAL FATHER OFTEN STANDS
> BETWEEN YOU AND DESTRUCTION
> AND IS WILLING TO RISK LOSING
> HIS REPUTATION FOR YOUR BETTERMENT.**

A spiritual father is willing to stand up for you, even though it may be at the expense of his own reputation. That depth of loyalty is so important to your success as a minister. God knows you need someone in your life who will help protect you from being destroyed by others — someone who is willing to lay his hand on your shoulder when others distance themselves from you.

That's one reason you must embrace your relationship with your spiritual father. He loves you enough to stick up for you. He is even willing to lose his own ministry so you can keep yours!

> **A SPIRITUAL FATHER IS WILLING TO LABOR WITH YOU AND TO WALK WITH YOU EVEN WHILE YOU'RE STILL UNQUALIFIED.**

Your spiritual father recognizes something within you that you don't even recognize in yourself. He sees the Lord working inside you.

In First Samuel 3, we can see this principle operating in the relationship between the elderly priest Eli and the young boy Samuel. One night the Lord spoke directly to Samuel rather than to Eli because the priest had failed to correct his sons when they committed great sin before Him.

When Samuel first heard God's voice, he went to Eli and said, "Here I am, for you called me." (Notice that the voice of God and the voice of Eli sounded exactly the same to Samuel. That's an important point to understand: The voice of a spiritual father will sound the same in your heart as the voice of the Holy Spirit.)

By the time Samuel had come to him the third time, Eli realized that the Lord was trying to communicate with the young boy. Before Samuel ever understood what God was doing in his life, Eli (who was Samuel's spiritual father) perceived the truth.

Then Eli told the young boy what he needed to do in order to flow with God's purposes for his life.

That's one of the roles of a spiritual father. He sticks with you and is willing to walk with you while you are still in your formative years, unqualified and unproven.

A SPIRITUAL FATHER ALLOWS YOU TO ECLIPSE HIM WHEN THE TIME COMES.

This is one of the most important principles of all in regard to the spiritual father-son relationship. You see, so many ministers live in dishonor because they want everyone to think that all they have accomplished, they have accomplished on their own.

But the truth is, no one ever accomplishes anything on his own. Someone is always responsible for helping a person attain the next goal in life.

Always remember that the reason you are where you are spiritually is that a father was willing to lay down his life in order to plant the seed of God's Word on the inside of you. That's why it is so important to have that person affirm you — to say, "Yes, that's the right thing for you to do" — when it is time for you to go the next level in ministry and become a spiritual father in other people's lives.

But remember — if the day comes when your ministry eclipses your spiritual father's ministry, God still desires for you to honor and esteem him. Your father should always hold the highest place of honor in your heart and your mind. Never forget him, for you can never replace his role in your life.

> **YOU ARE NOT RELEASED TO STEP OUT INTO THAT WHICH GOD HAS CALLED YOU TO DO UNTIL YOUR FATHER SAYS IT IS TIME.**

Despite all your gifts, skills, talents, ability, and preparation, you are not ready to launch out and fulfill the call of God on your life until your spiritual father voices his approval.

Think about it. Jesus was never released unto His Sonship until His Father spoke over Him (Heb. 5:4,5). The apostle Paul also wasn't released unto his ministry as an apostle to the Gentiles until his spiritual fathers spoke forth the word of the Lord over him:

> **Now in the church that was at Antioch there were certain prophets and teachers: Barnabas, Simeon who was called Niger, Lucius of Cyrene, Manaen who had been brought up with Herod the tetrarch, and Saul.**
> **As they ministered to the Lord and fasted, the Holy Spirit said, "Now separate to Me Barnabas and Saul for the work to which I have called them."**
> **Then, having fasted and prayed, and laid hands on them, they sent them away.**

So, being sent out by the Holy Spirit, they went down to Seleucia, and from there they sailed to Cyprus.

Acts 13:1-4

You see, the Holy Ghost doesn't *compete* with the people who are over you in the Lord. The Holy Ghost is *confirmed* and *complemented* by them.

A spiritual father knows things about you that you don't know. He can see the strong points in your life when you can't see them. He can also see the blind spots in your life that are hidden to you. He has a much better idea than you do of just how ready you really are. That's why God will use your father to help you know when the days of preparation are over and the time has come to step out.

Having identified the nature of a true spiritual father, we now need to look at several principles that, when followed, will put you in the category of a wise son.

A WISE SON KNOWS THAT HIS FATHER IS A CRUCIAL KEY TO HIS FUTURE.

The outcome of your future ministry is tied into how you respond to what your spiritual father says to you. As Proverbs 10:1 says, **"A wise son makes a glad father, but a foolish son is the grief of his mother."**

A WISE SON REALIZES THAT HE WILL BE PROMOTED IF HE IS REMAINS FAITHFUL.

You never need to wonder whether or not your father will promote you. He cannot fail to promote you when you're faithful. Why? Because it's an unchangeable law established in God's Word. Jesus said if you're faithful in that which is another man's, you will receive that which is your own. He also said if you're unfaithful over little, you will be unfaithful over much (Luke 16:10-12).

A WISE SON STICKS CLOSE TO HIS FATHER.

If you stay in close proximity to your father, blessings and finances will come to you.

Let me give you an illustration. I have some wonderful people who work for Linda and me in the ministry and have chosen to knit themselves closely to us. These people often reap the benefits of that deliberate choice.

For instance, there have been times when I've handed an individual some money and said, "Listen, I want you to take this money and get whatever you need. I want you to be able to focus on me and this ministry, not on what you don't have. Therefore, I'm going to do all I can to take the obstacles out of your life so you can become everything God has called you to become."

Because of these people's decision to stick close to me and Linda, God meets their needs one way or another. They don't have to fend for themselves.

Similarly, your needs will be taken care of as you stick close to *your* spiritual father. You don't need to worry about what you don't have. When you stick close to the delegated authority God has placed in your life, you have to be rewarded. After all, God's Word is on the line!

A WISE SON NEVER PANICS BECAUSE HE KNOWS THAT HIS FATHER WILL GIVE HIM WISDOM TO DEFEAT HIS ENEMIES.

Listen closely to what your spiritual father tells you, for he is often God's instrument in bringing Luke 21:15 to pass in your life: **"For I will give you a mouth and wisdom which all your adversaries** [both natural and spiritual] **will not be able to contradict or resist."**

A WISE SON IS KEENLY AWARE THAT IN ORDER TO POSSESS, HE MUST PURSUE.

Remember this: Your father doesn't need to know what *you* know. No matter how much you know, you need to know what *your father* knows. Therefore, it's your responsibility to pursue his wisdom with all your heart. Find out what it takes to draw out of your father the wisdom you need to unlock your future.

> **A WISE SON KNOWS THAT PEOPLE LISTEN TO HIM BECAUSE OF HIS RELATIONSHIP WITH HIS FATHER.**

The reason Joshua didn't have trouble leading the children of Israel was that the people esteemed his relationship with Moses. You see, a wise son understands that people listen to him because of the wisdom imparted into his life by his spiritual father. Therefore, the son should continue to honor his father and make his name great long after he, the student, has come into his own.

> **A WISE SON KNOWS THAT HIS FATHER IS MORE INTERESTED IN HIS SON'S SUCCESS THAN IN HIS APPROVAL.**

A true father is more interested in his son's success than in whether or not his son likes him. His attitude should be, "I don't care if you like me, Son, but you *are* going to win. I'm not called to your life to be your pal. My 'pal department' is already full. I'm called to teach you how to overcome every obstacle so you can become all that God has called you to be!"

> **A WISE SON WILL CONTINUE TO PURSUE HIS FATHER WHEN OTHERS HAVE LONG GONE.**

Elisha is the perfect example of this principle. Remember, we talked about Elisha earlier. After all the sons of the prophets were long gone, Elisha continued to pursue Elijah. He told the older prophet, "As long as you live and as long as the Lord lives, I will never leave you. I will not. Don't even try to make me!" (2 Kings 2:2).

Of course, a father must always put in front of his son the opportunity to leave him if he so chooses. But a wise son says, "As long as you live and as long as the Lord lives, I will never leave you."

As a wise son, you shouldn't look for a blessing; you should look for an *inheritance*, and the inheritance is never given until after the father is gone. But if you leave before the inheritance comes, you've lost your claim to it. All you did was waste your time, other than possibly gaining some valuable knowledge.

So stick close to your spiritual father. Earnestly pursue his wisdom, and diligently follow his counsel. And even if one day your ministry eclipses his, never stop honoring him in front of others and sowing blessing into his life!

PRINCIPLES FOR ESTEEMING THE VALUE OF A SPIRITUAL FATHER

✶ **A spiritual father is never a person whose advice you *look for*; he is a person whose advice you *follow*.**

✶ **A spiritual father is willing to take responsibility for your wrongdoing — to pay the** price when you don't possess the currency that is required in any given situation.

* A spiritual father often stands between you and destruction and is willing to risk losing his reputation for your betterment.

* A spiritual father is willing to labor with you and to walk with you even while you're still unqualified.

* A spiritual father allows you to eclipse him when the time comes.

* You are not released to step out into that which God has called you to do until your father says it is time.

* A wise son knows that his father is a crucial key to his future.

* A wise son realizes that he will be promoted if he is remains faithful.

* A wise son sticks close to his father.

* A wise son never panics because he knows that his father will give him wisdom to defeat his enemies.

* A wise son is keenly aware that in order to possess, he must pursue.

★ A wise son knows that people listen to him because of his relationship with his father.

★ A wise son knows that his father is more interested in his son's success than in his approval.

★ A wise son will continue to pursue his father when others have long gone.

NOTES:

_____

_____

_____

_____

_____

_____

_____

_____

_____

_____

_____

_____

_____

NOTES:

_____

_____

_____

_____

_____

_____

_____

_____

_____

_____

_____

_____

_____

_____

_____

_____

_____

_____

_____

_____

CHAPTER SIX

RELATING TO OTHERS WITH EXCELLENCE

Your ministry must be worked out among the imperfect — among those who, just like you, are on their way to perfection. That is an important point to keep in mind as you relate to the people you minister to or work with. If you're not careful, you can start thinking negatively about people as those imperfections crop up.

However, God has provided you with a solution to that problem. It's found in Proverbs 4:20,21:

> **My son, give attention to my words; incline your ear to my sayings.**
> **Do not let them depart from your eyes; keep them in the midst of your heart.**

God wants you to hear what He has already said in His Word. He also wants you to hear what He is speaking to your heart on an ongoing basis. He doesn't want you to think anything except what He has said about you and about those you relate to every day. God is telling you in this scripture, "Just keep what

I have told you before your eyes and in your heart. Don't listen to any other junk!"

Why does God ask this of you? Because His words are life to you when you find them and health to all your flesh (v. 22). You can only become a minister of excellence as you allow the paintbrush of God's Word to paint on the inside of you *His* perception of you and of the people you interact with on a daily basis.

Relating to Those You Minister To

So let's use the paintbrush of God's Word to paint your heart with some more principles of excellence. These particular principles are designed to help you relate correctly to the people you minister to.

> **AN EXCELLENT MINISTER IS ALWAYS MORE INTERESTED IN WHAT SOMEONE NEEDS TO HEAR THAN IN WHAT HE WANTS TO SAY.**

Jesus said that there is no greater love a man could ever display than that he lay down his life for his friends (John 15:13). If you're willing to call someone a friend, you have to be willing to say what he needs to hear.

So always preach the entire Word of God. Don't leave things out of the Word that may be unpopular with some of your listeners. You can't just say words that are comfortable for you to speak and comfortable for people to hear. You have to speak the message from Heaven that is "in due season" and then leave the outcome in God's hands.

AN EXCELLENT MINISTER REFUSES TO ENCOURAGE MEDIOCRITY.

If a mediocre person is rewarded with encouragement, he will never excel. Why is that? Because he knows he has nothing better coming if he changes.

I've been accused at times for not being very encouraging to people. Just recently I came to the revelation that I am actually very encouraging. You see, there is a difference between an encourager and someone who refuses to face problems in the lives of those under his authority. An encouraging person doesn't necessarily encourage people's *actions*; he encourages people's *hearts*.

If a person never comes to the realization in his heart that he needs to change, there is no way in the world you can ever encourage him. That kind of person is never going to change, no matter what. Instead, he will expect everyone else around him to change.

But something happens the moment a person realizes within himself, *God has shown me that I need to change in this area of my life, so I'm going to let Him change me.* No matter what condition that person's life is in, you can begin encouraging him as soon as he comes to that self-realization. You can tell him, "God loves you, and so do I. He's forgiven you, and so have I. I'll help you achieve the full level of repentance in your life. I'll be there for you as you start on the road to excellence."

Just as you are never to encourage mediocrity in others, you must also never allow mediocrity to take over an area of your life. If you don't walk in excellence, how can you expect anyone else around you to walk in excellence?

You'll never succeed in ministry if you attempt to exercise what is true in another person's life without first exercising what is true in yours. Before you preach the Word, you must first make sure you and your family members are living it yourselves.

So lead by example, never tolerating a "just-good-enough" performance from yourself. As you walk in excellence, you'll cause those under you to rise to the challenge and follow your example.

The voice of the Lord is calling His people to attention, to a deeper life of commitment. For those who heed that call, a "just-good-enough" attitude just won't be good enough anymore! These believers will no longer tolerate mediocrity in their lives, having finally realized that a casual attitude toward life leads only to failure and defeat.

Given this divine call to a deeper commitment, I can't imagine the unfaithfulness of a minister who would preach to people the Word of God and then never make sure that they apply it to their lives. A true minister doesn't let himself or others get away with the excuse "I'm trying to do what the Word says." There is no "trying" in the Bible — only *obeying*.

In the Kingdom of God, the coward always comes in last. I'm talking about the minister who doesn't want to hurt anyone's feelings. We often call a minister like that a "nice guy," but in reality, he's a coward because *a person will never be able to change what he is unwilling to confront.*

Think about Jesus' ministry for a moment. Every time Jesus opened His mouth, He had a purpose in mind. He might have started out sounding nice, but every one of His sermons stung in the end. Jesus even went so far at times as to call some of His listeners hypocrites, snakes, and white-washed tombs!

Personally, I wonder if I would have done well listening to that kind of message all the time. I probably would have sat there and thought, *I know exactly what Jesus is about to say. He's sounding good right now, but He's going to get us in a minute!*

Modern-day ministers would do well to look to Jesus as their Example in this area. Ministers have focused on telling people that if they would just believe God for a miracle, somehow a miracle would make things better for them. However, ministers often fail to add a very important point: *God cannot steer a ship in dry dock.* In other words, God can't change people who are stubborn and unapproachable because of their pride. He is hindered from moving on their behalf because they refuse to receive instruction.

You see, you have to bring people to a place in their walk with God where they are no longer just gathering information. The pursuit of excellence in

God has to become their very breath and life. That must be your goal as a minister of excellence. It can never be anything less if you want to stay faithful to your call.

> **AN EXCELLENT MINISTER REALIZES THAT**
> **HE ISN'T CALLED TO *REPLACE* GOD,**
> **BUT TO *RELEASE* GOD**
> **INTO THE LIVES OF OTHERS.**

Many modern-day ministers seem to "grade Christians on a curve." If a Christian lives a little bit better than everyone else, they label him as a great Christian. These ministers give the impression that God's Word is full of electives. If people want to ignore some of God's more difficult commandments, that's okay — as long as they're being obedient in most areas of their lives.

But God is a self-definer. He doesn't require from His people what *you* say; He requires from them what *He* says. Therefore, in your ministry you need to allow God to define what it means to be a true child of God; never try to create that definition yourself.

In Deuteronomy 10:12, the Bible gives us a good idea of what God requires of His people:

> **"And now, Israel, what does the Lord your God require of you, but to fear the Lord your God, to walk in all His ways and to love Him, to serve the Lord your**

God with all your heart and with all your soul."

Joshua 22:5 confirms this message:

But take diligent heed to do the commandment and the law, which Moses the servant of the Lord charged you, to love the Lord your God, and to walk in all his ways, and to keep his commandments, and to cleave unto him, and to serve him with all your heart and with all your soul.

Teach people to love God with all their heart and with all their soul. Show them how to go to another level, even if their flesh doesn't like it.

Now, loving God with all your heart is easy. The difficult challenge is loving Him with all your *soul*. But that isn't the end of it. Jesus takes it one step further in Matthew 22:37:

Jesus said to him, "You shall love the Lord your God with all your heart, with all your soul, and with all your mind."

A person can love God with his heart, and he can even tell you that he loves God with his soul. But the words that come out of his mouth will tell you whether or not he loves Him with his *mind*.

Then in John 6:53, Jesus takes God's requirements to a whole new level:

"...Most assuredly, I say to you, unless you eat the flesh of the Son of Man and drink His blood, you have no life in you."

You see, people need to know that the closer they get to God's will, the more He requires from them. They have to press into God with their entire being, or they will never experience the fullness of all He has planned for them.

Many of the disciples who heard Jesus make this statement couldn't handle it. They said, **"...This is a hard saying; who can understand it?"** (John 6:60). As a result, many of them stopped following Jesus from that day forward (v. 66).

So let God define what a Christian is. Don't try to replace His requirements with your own ideas; *release* God in people's lives by teaching them how to rise a higher level of excellence in Him!

One important aspect of taking people to a higher level in God is your responsibility to *teach them how to delight in worshiping God*.

Too many Christians want to separate worship from the house of God. But Jesus didn't separate worshiping from the church. Neither did the psalmist in Psalm 26:8, who said, **"Lord, I have loved the habitation of Your house, and the place where Your glory dwells."**

This psalmist loved to go to church! To him, church wasn't a place to get together with other believers in order to gossip or challenge authority. It was a play to get together and *worship*.

The Body of Christ in America has a real problem today. People have been given the impression that they can have church by watching a television program or listening to a teaching tape series. But it is impossible for anyone to become a mature Christian solely through television, books, or cassettes. Jesus didn't do it. Paul didn't do it.

Why is this? Because *spiritual growth is based on personal relationships*. You see, it's easy for people to say they believe something when they don't have to walk it out interacting with other people. Everything flows smoothly in a person's Christian walk until he meets another Christian!

So never allow people to separate their worship of God from the house of God. I'm not saying a person cannot worship God at home or wherever he is. But as a minister, you must make sure that you uphold the standard of Hebrews 10:25: Obedient children of God are never to forsake the assembling of themselves together as active members of a local body.

> AN EXCELLENT MINISTER DOESN'T WASTE
> HIS TIME WITH "TIME THIEVES."

Jesus said that **"...wisdom is justified by her children"** (Matt. 11:19). Wisdom is always justified by its product, not by its voice. That means if you want to know whether or not a person is really wise, look at the fruit of his life.

As a whole, the Body of Christ hasn't done that. Christians have often reduced wisdom down to what a person says. But wisdom is so much more than that. It isn't a matter of useless tidbits of information to talk about; it is divine knowledge imparted for the purpose of *action*.

Don't waste your time with people who just want to talk, because you'll come back twenty years later, and they'll still just be talking. I call people like that "time thieves." They steal your time, which is the most precious commodity you have. These people want you to spend more and more time counseling them with the wisdom God has given to you from the Word, but they have no intention of ever acting on what you tell them.

So fool-proof your life by getting rid of the time thieves. Quit spending ninety percent of your time with less than ten percent of the people. Time thieves will never produce anything no matter how much you put into them, and you don't have twenty years to waste trying to convince them to produce. Therefore, find people who *want* to produce fruit in their lives, and invest your time in them.

Also, be careful of people who constantly tell you how loyal they are to you and how much they love you. People do what they believe. You don't have to listen to what comes out of their mouths. Just pay attention to the fruit in their lives.

I watch out for people who are always telling me, "I'm really loyal, Pastor. I think you're really great." I just put people like that on probation in my mind because so many times I've seen them eventually rip up themselves and other people with strife and division before they finally leave the church.

That's why James 1:22 says, **"But be doers of the word, and not hearers only, deceiving yourselves."** Who is the biggest fool? The one who fools himself.

So don't trust people's words; trust their actions. Live your life listening with your eyes.

Personally, I don't listen to people who just talk. I invest my time in those who don't tell you one thing and do another. I'm out searching for the real — for the person of integrity who is through and through what he presents himself to be.

> **AN EXCELLENT MINISTER IS CONTINUALLY TEACHING OTHERS HOW TO MOVE OUT OF *CONVERSATION* INTO *DEMONSTRATION*.**

Matthew 15:8 tells us that God isn't looking for people who just give lip service: **"These people draw near to Me with their mouth, and honor Me with their lips, but their heart is far from Me."**

Therefore, it is imperative that you move out of just talking about excellence and begin to continually act on the words you speak. Check up on yourself continually to make sure you're not just spewing off words. Never talk about anything that you're not willing to immediately do, and teach others to do the same.

It's very difficult for people to break the chain of hearing the Word and not doing it once they have made a habit of it for a period of time. They learn to log things in their minds as an intellectual exercise. As they get smarter and smarter, they begin to sit back and compile a mental report card on your sermon rather than to consider how they can apply the scriptural principles to their own lives. These people are only interested in what they think, *not* what you think.

Your challenge as a minister is to teach people how to break this bad habit of hearing and never doing. Show them how to form a new habit of immediately acting on what they hear. It will lead them straight out of self-deception into certain success!

**AN EXCELLENT MINISTER CONCENTRATES
ON MINISTERING TO THOSE WHO DRAW
FROM THE ANOINTING ON HIS LIFE.**

Proverbs 20:5 gives you an excellent guideline to follow when choosing the people you should spend the most time ministering to:

Counsel [or wisdom] **in the heart of man is like deep water, but a man of understanding will draw it out.**

According to this scripture, *you can recognize the people you should spend time with by what they draw out of you.*

When I get around some people, nothing happens. But then I'll spend time with other individuals and find myself saying profound truths I've never heard before! Why? Because the second group of people draw out the anointing that resides within me.

I remember some individuals who called themselves my sons in the Lord but didn't act the part. These people only seemed to draw anger out of me by the things they did. They would say the right words, but then they wouldn't come through with the right performance. Or they would say the right things but then would always require a personal audience with me.

Rather than grabbing on to my instruction and then going forward on their own initiative, these particular individuals continually asked to spend time with me so I could instruct them in greater detail. As a result, they continually succeeded in drawing the wrong thing out of me, such as irritation and frustration.

But I have other sons in the faith who constantly draw out the wisdom on the inside of me. These are what Proverbs 20:5 calls "men of understanding." These are the individuals I desire to spend time with.

An excellent minister looks
for *multipliers*, not *hiders*.

The parable of the talents in Matthew 25:14-30 contains a very important principle. One servant was given five talents and then doubled his investment to ten talents. Another servant was given two talents and doubled those two to make four talents. These servants were *multipliers*. But the servant who was given one talent was a *hider*. He just hid that talent in the ground. His failure to multiply what he had been given earned him nothing but a stern rebuke from his master.

So be careful not to be like that third servant. Don't make the mistake many ministers do by spending a lot of time with people you shouldn't be close to just because you think they need you. You are to draw toward *multiplication*, not toward *need*. God has never told you to veer from the original commandment He gave man to "Be fruitful and multiply" (Gen. 1:22).

People think that God was telling Adam and Eve, "Get pregnant and have children." But that isn't what God said. He said, *"Be fruitful."* Galatians 5:22 provides a clearer idea of what God was talking about when it says, **"But the fruit of the Spirit is love...."** You see, the first commandment Adam and Eve walked out of was *love*. The moment they walked out of love, they immediately became fruitless.

Fruit always multiplies. However, there is only one way to bear fruit in your ministry — by drawing from the life and strength of the true Vine, Jesus: **"I am the vine, you are the branches. He who abides in Me, and I in him, bears much fruit; for without Me you can do nothing"** (John 15:5). As you draw life from Him, others can draw His life from you — and thus, the multiplication process begins.

But notice that God added something else to His instructions to Adam and Eve in Genesis 1:28 (*KJV*): **"...Be fruitful, and multiply, AND REPLEN-ISH...."**

You see, the relationships God wants you to focus on are the ones you have with people who multiply and replenish the virtue they draw out of you. I call this *the law of replenished virtue* in relationships.

This law is illustrated in Mark 5:25-34, where we find the account of the woman with the issue of blood. Jesus was walking along, thronged by a great multitude of people. Yet when the woman with the issue of blood crept up to Him and touched the hem of His garment, Jesus looked around and asked, "Who touched Me?"

The disciples replied, "Master, *everyone* is touching You and pushing on You in this crowd!"

"No," Jesus said, "Someone touched Me *in faith*. Virtue has gone out of Me."

"What are You talking about, Jesus? You know that everyone is pulling on You."

"No, you don't even know what I'm talking about. Someone did something different."

So Jesus kept looking around, asking, "Who is it? Who is it?" Immediately the woman realized that Jesus knew they had connected, so she came and told Him everything. As she spoke of her healing with humble gratitude, Jesus was replenished in the virtue that had been taken out of Him.

You see, virtue is only replenished in relationship by *gratitude*. But many people are *not* thankful; therefore, the virtue they draw out of you is never replenished. This kind of relationship begins to wear you down rather than to build you up.

If you have a lot of relationships that don't fulfill the law of replenished virtue, your anointing will continue to be drained away until you finally run out. So watch out for people who continually drain you, my friend. You'll recognize them as soon as you start talking to them. It isn't a privilege or a pleasure to talk to people like that; it is an unnecessary commitment that costs dearly and deeply.

Remember, Proverbs 11:25 (*NIV*) says, **"A generous man will prosper; he who refreshes others will himself be refreshed."** To be effective in ministry, you must not only minister to people who draw from the anointing upon your life, but who also bring encouragement, blessing, and refreshing to *you*. These are the relationships that will eventually produce multiplied fruit for the Kingdom.

So spend time with the people who take what you give them and multiply it. The more you give these fruitful people, the more they will multiply what they have been given to produce an abundant harvest to the glory of God.

AN EXCELLENT MINISTER KNOWS HE CANNOT HELP THOSE WHO THINK THAT THEY KNOW MORE THAN HE DOES.

You can't help a person who thinks he knows it all. This type of person may keep coming to you to ask questions. But every time he asks you a question, you can tell he already thinks he knows the answer better than you do — and you haven't even opened your mouth yet!

In that case, it is best to say, "You know what, Brother? I'm not going to argue with you about that subject. You think you already know the answer, so let's just leave it at that."

You see, you have been called to bring correction into the lives of those God has placed under you (Prov. 9:8,9). But whereas correction from the top is just, correction from below is rebellion.

In Numbers 12, Miriam and Aaron rebelled against Moses, trying to correct him from their position under his authority. Then in Numbers 16, Korah rebelled against Moses because he didn't agree with his leadership. What was the result of the rebellion of these three people? They all received the judgment of God to differing degrees.

Correction from the top is just. If you don't correct people who are under you as God has called you to do, you do them a great disservice.

So don't spend your time with people who act like they know more than you do. Concentrate on people who *exercise receiving* — who are growing as they act on the Word they hear.

The individual who *isn't* exercising receiving may still come asking for your advice. However, the entire time you're talking with this person, you'll know on the inside that you're wasting your time because he'll never do one thing you're telling him to do. This type of person just wants to find someone to say what he wants to hear so he can do what he wants to do. That way he'll have someone to blame when things don't work out!

You can't help people unless they become willing to let you inside their hearts where you can begin to take down the walls that were erected long ago. These are the people who will come back to you later and show you the fruit they have borne for the Kingdom of God.

> **AN EXCELLENT MINISTER NEVER REVEALS HIS WEAKNESSES TO THE ONES HE TEACHES.**

You must never reveal your weaknesses to the people under you until you have helped them grow to the place where they are no longer servants. Once they have gained the character and spiritual maturity that allows you to call them friends, you can begin to allow them access to your heart.

Consider the earthly ministry of Jesus. It was in the Garden of Gethsemane that Jesus revealed for the first time to His disciples the way He really felt:

Then He said to them, "My soul is exceedingly sorrowful, even to death. Stay here and watch with Me."

Matthew 26:38

Until that time, Jesus never told His disciples what He was thinking. But right before they left for the Garden of Gethsemane, Jesus told His disciples:

"No longer do I call you servants, for a servant does not know what his master is doing; but I have called you friends, for all things that I heard from My Father I have made known to you."

John 15:15

Until Jesus called someone who was under Him a friend — until that person received a promotion — He never revealed His inner struggles to him. As a minister of excellence, you need to follow Jesus' example.

> AN EXCELLENT MINISTER WORKS DILIGENTLY
> TO HELP HIS SPIRITUAL SONS
> BECOME GREATER THAN HIMSELF.

Always strive to make those you are responsible for greater than you are. Remember, they are starting out with the seed that has taken you a long time to gather. As that seed blossoms and brings forth fruit, it will go on to affect the next generation for the Kingdom of God in an even greater way than you can because revelation continues to grow and expand as time passes.

Relating to Those
Who Work Under You

Now let's look at some principles that are designed to help you relate correctly to the people who work under your authority. These people are the ones who work closely with you on a daily basis; therefore, the way you relate to them is an essential part of fulfilling your call to the ministry in excellence.

**AN EXCELLENT MINISTER REALIZES
THE BOUNDARIES OF HIS OWN LIMITATIONS.**

One of the biggest challenges you will ever face as a minister is avoiding the pitfall of spreading yourself too thin as you take on the responsibilities of ministry. Therefore, you must take the time to evaluate and understand your limitations; then you can become excellent in fulfilling the responsibilities God has given *you* instead of thinking you have to handle every task in sight.

You see, the more tasks you try to handle on your own, the less effective you will be at everything you attempt to do. That's why you have to refuse to try to do everything yourself. Allow other people to fulfill the roles they are called to fulfill in your life. You'll never know who God wants to use to create a greater future for you if you're always making yourself the only one who serves.

It's up to you to realize your limitations; to set borders around those limitations; and then to begin to live inside those limitations. Stop worrying about what may happen if you delegate certain areas of responsibility to others. God doesn't want you to burn yourself out in the ministry; He only wants you to do what He has called *you* to do.

AN EXCELLENT MINISTER IS ABLE TO DISCOVER
THE HIDDEN GIFTS THAT LIVE
INSIDE THE PEOPLE WHO SURROUND HIM.

Once you draw the borders of your limitations, you have to realize that the gifts you lack are living on the inside of someone else in your sphere of influence. Your job is to discover those hidden gifts and to help bring them forth so they can bless the Body of Christ.

If a minister tries to do too much in his ministry, he begins to dwarf the growth of other people around him. In fact, he actually becomes an enemy of God's work in their lives.

Don't be guilty of that same mistake. As a minister of excellence, learn to delight in letting people use and exercise their God-given gifts!

**AN EXCELLENT MINISTER NEVER GIVES ANYONE
THE RESPONSIBILITY OVER THE ISSUES
FOR WHICH HE ALONE IS RESPONSIBLE.**

You should always look for areas of responsibility to delegate to others according to their gifts and strengths. However, there are certain issues that you alone are responsible for in your life and ministry. No one else can deal with those issues but you, because they are between you and God. He isn't going to talk to another person about those issues for the rest of eternity.

Therefore, you need to protect those responsibilities. Make sure other people keep their opinions away from them. People who work under your authority shouldn't even think about your own personal and ministerial responsibilities. The moment they start thinking about them, they aren't doing what they were asked to do.

**AN EXCELLENT MINISTER CONTINUALLY RAISES
THE PERFORMANCE LEVEL OF THOSE AROUND HIM.**

As a person of excellence, you aren't competing with anyone, nor are you trying to impress anyone. But just by being who you are, you raise the level of the people who work with you. You lift the standards; you increase the vision. The way you respond excellently to every situation is the way you influence those around you to respond.

All you have to do is take a look at my church staff, and you'll see what I mean. They don't look like any other staff you've ever seen! They carry themselves differently. They talk differently. When someone walks in the church building, he says, "These people look sharp! I've never seen a church staff look this good!"

So make sure your staff maintains the same standards of excellence that you yourself hold in life. Let them know that there are certain things you just will not accept — certain things that are unacceptable in the arena of dress, in the arena of being on time, in the arena of behavior. Remember, people can't stay in the presence of excellence and not change!

AN EXCELLENT MINISTER KNOWS WHO IS ASSIGNED
TO HIS LIFE BUT IS MORE KEENLY AWARE
OF THOSE WHO ARE NOT.

Remember this: Many people will come to you and ask to work with you. But how they respond to what you say to them will determine whether or not they've been assigned to your life. Are they argumentative? Do they challenge you? What do they do with your instructions after they leave your presence? Unless you see that a person hears and acts on what you say, you can rest assured — that person has not been assigned to you.

You can always tell the people who shouldn't be on your church staff by the divisiveness and disunity they bring into any given situation. Every time some people walk into a room, others in the room think apprehensively, *Oh, no, look who's here.* Instead of introducing a solution, these people always seem to introduce a bigger problem.

But here is an important point to consider: Is there anyone on your staff who never seems to listen to you? If so, I'll tell you why that may be so. That person may not be listening to you because at some point in the past, you didn't listen to God concerning his or her role in your life.

You see, situations like this are often the result of the law of sowing and reaping in operation. People who don't listen to you may be the fruit of bad seed that you once sowed in your own life. God gave you an instruction, but you didn't do it. Now you give someone an instruction, and they don't do it. As Galatians 6:7 says, whatever a man sows, that is what he will reap. As long as the earth remains, seedtime and harvest will never cease (Gen. 8:22).

Remember, you are here on this earth for the same reason that Jesus came to earth: *to do the will of Him who sent you* (John 5:30). You are not to have an opinion about God's will. You're not here to figure out whether you like it or whether you don't. If God has already said in His Word, "This is the way it is" — then that's just the way it is!

When you live this way every day of your life, the law of sowing and reaping goes into operation to your benefit. You are then able to form a team that yields great productivity because all team members will always perform the tasks that are requested of them.

> **AN EXCELLENT MINISTER CHOOSES TO SPEAK GOOD WORDS CONCERNING THOSE HE HAS CHOSEN TO WALK THROUGH LIFE WITH.**

You must stay positive about the people you work with in the ministry. You must choose to believe in the team you've put together by giving each staff member a portion of your time, your love, your dedication, and your understanding.

Never stop believing in the team you're on. Always be willing to share your appreciation for them and your gratitude for their help in the ministry.

There is no doubt about it, friend — relationships are the key to an excellent ministry. But it isn't just a matter of learning how to relate correctly to those God has placed under your care. You first have to discern who *is* and who *is not* assigned to you.

As the old saying goes, "The proof is in the pudding." That means you have to get beyond people's words and start hunting for the fruit of obedience.

Principles for Relating to Those You Minister To

✳ An excellent minister is always more interested in what someone needs to hear than in what he wants to say.

✳ An excellent minister refuses to encourage mediocrity.

✳ An excellent minister realizes that he isn't called to *replace* God, but to *release* God into the lives of others.

✳ An excellent minister doesn't waste his time with "time thieves."

✳ An excellent minister is continually teaching others how to move out of *conversation* into *demonstration.*

✳ An excellent minister concentrates on ministering to those who draw from the anointing on his life.

✳ An excellent minister looks for *multipliers,* not *hiders.*

✳ An excellent minister knows he cannot help those who think that they know more than he does.

✳ An excellent minister never reveals his weaknesses to the ones he teaches.

★ An excellent minister works diligently to help his spiritual sons become greater than himself.

PRINCIPLES FOR RELATING TO THOSE WHO WORK UNDER YOU

★ An excellent minister realizes the boundaries of his own limitations.

★ An excellent minister is able to discover the hidden gifts that live inside the people who surround him.

★ An excellent minister never gives anyone the responsibility over the issues for which he alone is responsible.

★ An excellent minister continually raises the performance level of those around him.

★ An excellent minister knows who is assigned to his life but is more keenly aware of those who are not.

★ An excellent minister chooses to speak good words concerning those he has chosen to walk through life with.

NOTES:

_____

_____

NOTES:

_____

_____

_____

_____

_____

_____

_____

_____

_____

_____

_____

_____

_____

_____

_____

_____

_____

_____

_____

_____

_____

_____

REPRESENTING JESUS WITH EXCELLENCE

You can only minister to people effectively when they can see evidence of God's hand on your life. People are looking to see if you represent Jesus well — if His promises are manifested on your behalf on an ongoing basis.

Every time you walk into a room, you should be representing Jesus with excellence:

- in your demeanor.
- in your words.
- in your appearance.
- in the attitudes you display.
- in the respect you show toward others.
- in the way you serve other people.
- in the ease in which you receive blessings from the Lord.

Therefore, I want to share with you some principles of excellence that will help you live as a worthy representative of Jesus in every aspect of your life.

AN EXCELLENT MINISTER SEES THE IMPORTANCE OF BEING CONSISTENT IN PERSONAL HYGIENE.

Don't make it your goal to just look presentable. You should want to be a person who looks inviting every moment that you're awake!

Why is personal hygiene so important? Well, consider this: Until the devil's lease on this earth is over, the Holy Spirit needs these bodies in which we live in order to perform God's will on the earth. That's why God's command in Romans 6:12,14 is so important:

> **Therefore do not let sin reign in your mortal body, that you should obey it in its lusts....**
> **For sin shall not have dominion over you, for you are not under law but under grace.**

Your body is the vessel through which God's perfect will is carried out in your life. So make this your constant prayer: *"Lord, what do You want to do with this body in which I live for the decades I have left on this earth? How can You use this vessel to obtain the glory and honor due Your Name?"*

As you ask God to reveal His perfect will, stand in faith for the Holy Spirit to minister to you exactly what you need to know. Then keep your body fit and prepared to carry out His will so He can receive the greatest glory possible through your own "earthen vessel."

You see, an important part of raising the standards of your life is the way you present yourself. You will never take a step up in life without dealing with your personal appearance. However, you'll find that, as you change on the inside, it will change the way you look on the outside.

Modern-day society has compromised on this issue of personal appearance by making it fashionable to wear loose-fitting clothes and thus help people become overweight. After all, when a person's clothes start getting uncomfortable and tight, that gives him great motivation to make some adjustments in eating habits!

I don't like it when my clothes get too tight. I start telling myself, *You know, I've been eating too much lately. I may be eating too much at the wrong time of day.* I speak to myself like that because I don't want to start sliding downhill with my personal appearance until, all of a sudden, I have a huge mountain to climb to get back to where I was before!

I've found that it is a lot easier to maintain my weight than it is to get heavy and then have to lose it. However, too many ministers don't even try to keep themselves fit as they get older.

Don't let yourself start down that downhill slope of getting overweight and out of shape. It's unhealthy to stay on a constant "gain weight-lose weight" cycle. It's just better all the way around to stay fit and maintain your ideal weight as much as possible.

It is my goal to look as good as I possibly can every single day. Now, I didn't grow up with a desire to pursue that goal. In fact, I wasn't raised with any understanding at all of how to maintain personal hygiene. That wasn't how we lived at home when I was a boy. In fact, I understood even as a teenager that if anything was going to happen in improving my personal hygiene, I was going to have to make it happen on my own.

Having never been taught about this subject, however, I didn't know how to go about improving my personal appearance. This is how totally ignorant I was: To clean my jeans, I'd sit in a bathtub of warm water and bleach with my jeans on! I just didn't know the right way to do it.

But something inside me told me that I didn't need to live my life as it had been lived before me. I could do something different; I could change. So ignorant or not, I started learning how to improve my personal appearance — a quest that goes on to this day!

I believe that no matter how much or how little you spend on clothing, you can still look fashionable. That doesn't mean you should go out of your way to follow fashion fads and look "trendy," but you *should* want to look fashionable. If you're spending a certain amount of money on clothes, you can either spend it on something that looks good or something that looks bad. Either way, the same amount of money is spent.

You may say, "But I don't know how to dress fashionably!" That's all right. Just get rid of your pride and start asking the advice of those who do know how to dress well!

I made the decision in my own life that since I wanted to become a person of excellence, I wasn't going to be ashamed to ask people how to improve myself. I'm not embarrassed to ask someone to teach me how to tie a tie. I'm not afraid to hear someone else tell me that I don't know how to fold my pocket silk. I want to learn how to maximize the good genes my momma and daddy gave me — and so should you!

No matter where you are on the scale of personal appearance, you can always take a step up. You can always become better. Let's take your hair as an example. If you've had the same hairstyle for the past twenty years, start looking at some new hairstyle possibilities. Go to the most contemporary hair salon you can find and discover a new hairstyle that goes well with the shape of your face.

Here's another important point on this issue: As a minister, I make it a point to always be "on" and never "off." After all, I never know when I'm going to be needed, so I always try to look my best. For instance, I rarely, if ever, undo my tie while I'm out in public. I never know when someone might stop me on the street looking for a professional to give a million dollars to!

So keep on looking for ways to improve your personal appearance. Maintain the attitude, "I am who I am. This is what I have to work with. But I'll tell you what — I'm never going to let myself become a slob, and I'll always make sure that I present myself as the best that I can be!"

AN EXCELLENT MINISTER CONTINUALLY UPGRADES HIS PERSONAL CHARACTER.

Make a commitment to continually search your heart, looking for ways to become better in the arena of character. Determine to continually be open to changing yourself, even when other people don't see anything that you need to change. Allow God to continually change you so you can attain God's highest and best for your life.

So many ministers don't make the development of personal character a priority in their lives. The closer you get to these ministers, the less character you see in them.

I don't want it to be that way with me. I want to continually upgrade my character — not because anyone is making me do it, but because I *choose* to do it. The closer people get to me, the more godly character I want them to see.

I want my congregation to have a pastor who is willing to pay the price so they can be everything God has called them to be. I want them to have someone leading them whom they can be proud of —

not someone who has to be threatened all the time in order to get him to move forward.

Keep that same desire burning in *your* heart. Internalize the truths you minister to others, and allow those truths to shut the valve of wrong and open the valve of godly excellence in your life.

> **AN EXCELLENT MINISTER IS A SELF-CORRECTOR.**

This is one of the most important things you can ever do as a minister. If you will continually and consistently correct yourself, no one else will ever have to come and correct you for the mistakes you've made.

Conduct checkups on yourself every day. Ask yourself, *What are the adjustments I need to make today to make myself a better minister and a better representative of Jesus?* Get on your knees and ask the Lord, "Father, what happened today that I need to change? How well did I treat the people I interacted with? How well did I treat those You have placed over me? How well did I treat those who are under my authority? How did I do today, Lord?"

As you stay sensitive to the Holy Spirit, He will begin to show you how to make immediate adjustments. You'll begin to catch yourself when you say something unkind in your conversations with people so you can immediately change what you're saying or the way you're saying it. Or you'll catch yourself doing something wrong and be able to change what you're doing right in the middle of the situation.

Have you been unkind? Have you failed to display the fruit of the Spirit? If so, adjust yourself as soon as you recognize what you've done. Why? Because you are a minister of excellence!

**AN EXCELLENT MINISTER REFUSES
TO LIE TO HIMSELF.**

The biggest fool you will ever run into is the fool who continually fools himself, because that individual is a hypocrite. He's the person who expects other people to follow a list of "do's and don'ts" that he doesn't even follow himself.

You see, you can become religious without ever becoming godly. You can do everything the church requires without ever doing anything *God* requires.

So always tell yourself the truth about yourself. When you're wrong, admit it. If you deal with yourself, God won't have to send a prophet to deal with you. Besides, you only have a right to expect other people to stand for the truth when you know you are standing for it yourself.

**AN EXCELLENT MINISTER IS A PERSON
OF DISCRETION WHO USES WISDOM
TO AVOID DAMAGING ATTITUDES,
WORDS, AND ACTIONS.**

Discretion is the finishing school of a minister's character. It's the finishing touch God puts on the life of a man or woman of God, and it is one of the greatest attributes any person can possess. A person of discretion is someone who is highly sought after because he knows when to speak and when not to speak. He also knows *how* to speak to people in any given situation.

You must continually pursue discretion, for it is the quality that helps you know how to respond in your relationships with others. You have to be able to go into any situation without fear, knowing that you will always be discreet in the way you respond to people. You will not say words you shouldn't say.

You see, words can kill or words can set a person free. Sometimes you must not say certain things, even if you know what you want to say is true. You have to know when to be discreet by keeping your mouth shut; how to be discreet in business matters; and how to be discreet about what is going on in the lives of the people you minister to.

A minister of discretion gives insightful counsel. He is able to mingle in a roomful of people without telling everything he knows because he is a person of restraint who realizes that only a fool speaks his whole mind.

A minister of discretion isn't secretive; he is a warm, open, and loving person. But he is also a person who knows how *not* to step over a line with what he says to others.

Recently someone said to me, "You know, Robb, I don't ever have to be apprehensive about taking you into any situation with any group of people, because I know you'll never hurt me." I considered that a high compliment, for that person had just described me as a man of discretion.

AN EXCELLENT MINISTER CRITICALLY CONSIDERS THE CONSEQUENCES HE MAY BRING INTO OTHER PEOPLE'S LIVES BY HIS DECISIONS.

As a person of discretion, you will begin to realize more and more that *what you do affects other people.* Let me say it another way: *The decisions you make bring consequences into the lives of others.*

Therefore, you have to start asking yourself before you speak, *What will my words mean to this person? How will they affect him?* Discretion will help you put yourself in the position of that other person. If you realize that what you're about to say will bring unnecessary pain to him, you should simply choose to keep quiet.

Romans 14:13 says, **"Therefore let us not judge one another anymore, but rather resolve this, not to put a stumbling block or a cause to fall in our brother's way."** In other words, if you ever do anything that hurts another person or causes him to sin, you must determine never to do it again.

Then in First Corinthians 10, the apostle Paul said something similar:

Give no offense, either to the Jews or to the Greeks or to the church of God,

just as I also please all men in all things, not seeking my own profit, but the profit of many, that they may be saved.

1 Corinthians 10:32,33

Paul was saying, "If anything I do causes another person to stumble, I'll never do it again. Even though all things are lawful for me, all things are not profitable to me. I'm not going to be brought under the power of anything that will adversely affect another person's life. Let it never be said that my freedom ever caused another person's bondage."

AN EXCELLENT MINISTER ALLOWS DISCRETION
TO CONTROL HIS DESTRUCTIVE EMOTIONS.

You see, when discretion is properly used, it will protect you. Discretion becomes a guard against emotions that can ultimately destroy your life.

Many ministers can tell other people what to do, but they can't do it themselves. These ministers possess a great deal of wisdom in giving counsel to others, yet they lack the ability to control their own emotions of fear, low self-esteem, frustration, or anger. In fact, their emotions have gotten them into more trouble than their bodies can get them out of!

Proverbs 19:11 tells you the way it should be in your life:

The discretion of a man makes him slow to anger, and his glory is to overlook a transgression.

The word for "discretion" in this verse is the Hebrew word *sekel*, which means *intelligence* or *prudence*. A person of great discretion and prudence can overlook another's transgression because he is slow to become angry and offended. He is in control of his emotions.

However, make sure you don't overlook things in your own life that shouldn't be overlooked. Tackle the areas of your life you need to tackle, and learn to control your destructive emotions. Remember, you will never change anything in life that you are unwilling to confront.

THE SUCCESS OF AN EXCELLENT MINISTER IS UNDENIABLY LINKED TO HIS HABITS AND ROUTINES.

What are the things you do most often every day? What gets your attention on a daily basis? How are you spending your time? What are you doing each day to build the future you want to build? These are the things that will determine your ultimate success or failure in life and ministry.

Your daily routines — the things you do over and over and over again on a daily basis — are keys to your success in life. If you put the right things into your daily life, you will be propelled toward your dream every step of the way. On the other hand, if you put the wrong things into your life every day, you will actually propel yourself toward failure and frustration — and that's a place in life you *don't* want to go.

Proverbs 29:18 (*KJV*) says, **"Where there is no vision, the people perish: but he that keepeth the law, happy is he."** That's why it's so important to establish routine responsibilities that are scriptural and that help you focus toward your ultimate goals. That is the surest way for your goals regarding success in ministry and in life to be realized.

> **AN EXCELLENT MINISTER KEEPS HIS WORD AND REFUSES TO COMPROMISE HIS PRINCIPLES.**

I am a person of principle. No matter what situation arises, I never compromise my principles for anyone. *Ever.* Why? Because I have to live with myself.

You see, life is real simple for me. I never commit myself partially to anything. If I say I'll do something, I don't contemplate the possibility of *not* doing it; I just do it.

Psalm 15:4 tells you that a righteous man swears to his own hurt and does not change. So never fail to keep your word to anyone. If you have to, swear to your own hurt.

Many times I have given my word about something that I later regretted. When it actually came time to keep my commitment, I almost couldn't do it.

If I could have turned my foot around, I'd have kicked my rear end all the way home for making that commitment! Nevertheless, I still kept my word, even in the face of pain. Why? Because I am a man of principle. I am determined to be faithful to do what I have said I will do.

You, too, should be a person of your word. If you said you would do something, then do it! In fact, as a minister of excellence, you must not only keep your word; you must also strive to *exceed* the commitment you have given to people!

You see, as soon as you begin to compromise your principles, you leave the playing field on which you know how to operate and enter someone else's playing field. Now all of a sudden you have put yourself in a bad position. You have to depend on someone else's perception of what is right and true in order to find success in life.

What's the solution? It's simple: *Never allow yourself to compromise your principles for anyone, anywhere, for any reason.*

AN EXCELLENT MINISTER WILL NOT
BE DISQUALIFIED BY SOMETHING AS SMALL AS
ANOTHER PERSON'S POOR ATTITUDES.

You must never respond to another person's flesh. Don't relate to other people according to the way they've spoken about you or treated you. Instead, relate to them according to the Word of

God. Hold on to what God tells you to do in each situation. Believe what He says about people, not what people say about themselves or about you.

Second Corinthians 5:16 gives us an important guideline regarding this issue:

Therefore, from now on, we regard no one according to the flesh. Even though we have known Christ according to the flesh, yet now we know Him thus no longer.

You see, I don't look at a person from a human point of view. I refuse to relate to that person according to his flesh. I'm going to relate to him according to his *spirit*. I refuse to become disqualified for the prize God has reserved for me just because of another person's flesh; I am going to relate to that person *according to the Word*. I choose to believe only what God says about me and about any other person I interact with in life.

In Psalm 119:165 (*KJV*), the psalmist says, **"Great peace have they which love thy law: and nothing shall offend them."** Then Jesus says in Mark 4:17 that offense comes *because of the Word*. In other words, offense comes to take the Word of God out of a person's heart, because the moment of offense is the moment that all forward motion stops.

As a minister of excellence, you must never allow yourself to become offended. Embrace the Word of God and what God has spoken through the pens of the apostles and prophets. Don't hold on to your own personal feelings, because the moment you take offense is the moment the Word of God no longer works in your life. You may still know what the Word says in your mind; you may still be able to quote it with your mouth. However, there will no longer be any power to the words you speak.

This is why you have to relate to God in your relationships with other people. Relating to people directly will only cause you to lower your standards of excellence as you yield to feelings of hurt, anger, and offense.

Take the time to test yourself every day to make sure the fruit of the spirit is working in your life. Give yourself regular checkups to see whether or not you are representing Jesus with excellence and ministering correctly according to God's Word. Then if you ever fail the test in any area — make sure you do something about it!

Embrace the Journey

Remember, my fellow minister, *excellence is a journey, not a destination.* So live with an inner drive to pursue excellence in the ministry every moment. Continually press on to the next level in your walk with God according to His command in Jeremiah 29:13: **"...You will seek Me and find Me, when you search for Me with all your heart."**

You will only possess what you are willing to pursue, especially when it comes to this particular journey. Success depends entirely on your passion for pursuit.

But you can do it, friend. You can wake up every morning with the thought, *How can I become a better Christian and a better minister today?* You can make today's excellence the mediocrity of tomorrow every day of your life!

Just determine that you will never be satisfied with the status quo. You will let go of yesterday's disappointments and continue to pursue, press, and *push* toward all that God has for you in the ministry. From this day forward, you're not going to let *anything* get in your way of the prize of your high calling in Christ!

PRINCIPLES FOR REPRESENTING JESUS WITH EXCELLENCE

✶ **An excellent minister sees the importance of being consistent in personal hygiene.**

✶ **An excellent minister continually upgrades his personal character.**

✶ **An excellent minister is a self-corrector.**

✶ **An excellent minister refuses to lie to himself.**

✶ **An excellent minister is a person of discretion who uses wisdom to avoid damaging attitudes, words, and actions.**

✶ **An excellent minister critically considers the consequences he may bring into other people's lives by his decisions.**

✶ An excellent minister allows discretion to control his destructive emotions.

✶ The success of an excellent minister is undeniably linked to his habits and routines.

✶ An excellent minister keeps his word and refuses to compromise his principles.

✶ An excellent minister will not be disqualified by something as small as another person's poor attitudes.

NOTES:

_____

_____

_____

_____

_____

_____

_____

_____

_____

_____

NOTES:

PRAYER OF SALVATION

Perhaps you have never been born again and therefore haven't even begun the pursuit of excellence in God. If you have never received Jesus Christ as your personal Lord and Savior and would like to do that right now, just pray this simple prayer:

Dear Lord Jesus, I know that I am lost and need Your forgiveness. I believe that You died for me on the Cross and that God raised You from the dead. I now invite You to come into my heart to be my Lord and Savior. Forgive me of all sin in my life and make me who You want me to be. Amen.

If you prayed this prayer from your heart, congratulations! You have just changed your destiny and will spend eternity with God. Your sins were forgiven the moment you made Jesus the Lord of your life. Now God sees you as pure and holy, as if you had never sinned. You have been set free from the bondage of sin!

God didn't call you to live a life of mediocrity.
He didn't create you to be "just good enough."

These books will guide you down the road to excellence
so that you can experience the extraordinary
and bask in God's best.
Make the quality decision to pursue
His standard of excellence in every area of your life!

ROBB THOMPSON

ROBB THOMPSON

ROBB THOMPSON

$^$5 #4023/Soft Cover $^$10 #4026/Soft Cover $^$25 #4024/Hard Cover

OTHER BOOKS
BY ROBB THOMPSON

Victory Over Fear

The Winning Decision

You Are Healed

Marriage From God's Perspective

The Great Exchange:
Your Thoughts for God's Thoughts

Winning the Heart of God

Excellence in the Workplace

Shattered Dreams

For a complete listing
of additional products
by Robb Thompson, please call:

1-877-WIN-LIFE
(1-877-946-5433)

You can also visit us on the web at:
www.winninginlife.org

To contact Robb Thompson, please write:

Robb Thompson
P. O. Box 558009
Chicago, Illinois 60655

Please include your prayer requests
and comments when you write.